GENERAL QUARTERS!

Memoirs of a WORLD WAR II veteran aboard the LSM-143

Ray McCoy

Foxhole Publishing, LLC, Tennessee

Foxhole Publishing, LLC
3046 Wayside Rd
Manchester, Tennessee 37355, USA

Copyright © 2016 Ray McCoy

Front Cover photograph: US Navy photo # NH 79857 from the
collections of the US Naval Historical Center

Back cover photo of Del: Family's personal collection
Back cover photo of typhoon: Taken by David Sweeten aboard the USS
Mona Island contributed by Henry Carr. Donation of David Sweeten
Family
Back cover photo of Kamikaze: US Naval Historical Center

ISBN: 978-0-9978855-0-7

Library of Congress Control Number: 2016912774

 View more stories, photos, audio interview snippets, and more on
our Facebook page: *https://www.facebook.com/usslsm143/*

Printed in the United States of America

HISTORY / Military / World War II / Naval

INTRODUCTION BY THE AUTHOR

I peered from the back pew of the Manchester Church of the Nazarene dodging the head of the person just in front of me to get a better look at the congregation. We were celebrating an early Veterans' Day that Sunday. Brother Jim Hodges began his service as always with song and prayer requests. Then he requested all veterans to stand and be recognized. We all offered a loud, enthusiastic round of applause when all the veterans stood. Many of the "recent" conflicts were represented: Korea, Vietnam, Desert Storm, and on and on. As I panned my eyes around the crowd, Del Garforth slowly, but proudly, rose from his usual front row seat as the pianist began to play. He was the last one to stand so he caught my attention right away. "Onward Christian Soldier" rang through the air as the assembly joined the chorus:

Onward, Christian soldiers, marching as to war,

   with the cross of Jesus going on before.

   Christ, the royal Master, leads against the foe;

   forward into battle see his banners go!

   Onward, Christian soldiers, marching as to war,

   with the cross of Jesus going on before.

i

General Quarters!

2.   At the sign of triumph Satan's host doth flee;

on then, Christian soldiers, on to victory!

Hell's foundations quiver at the shout of praise;

brothers, lift your voices, loud your anthems raise.

3.   Like a mighty army moves the church of God;

brothers, we are treading where the saints have trod.

We are not divided, all one body we,

one in hope and doctrine, one in charity.

4.   Crowns and thrones may perish,

kingdoms rise and wane,

but the church of Jesus constant will remain.

Gates of hell can never gainst that church prevail;

we have Christ's own promise, and that cannot fail.

5.   Onward then, ye people, join our happy throng,

blend with ours your voices in the triumph song.

Glory, laud, and honor unto Christ the King,

this through countless ages men and angels sing.

Introduction by the Author

That same song also resonated at the funeral of American president and Allied Supreme Commander Dwight D. Eisenhower in March 1969.

Winston Churchill chose this very hymn at a church service after he and Franklin Roosevelt met in August 1941 on the battleship HMS Prince of Wales to agree upon the terms of the Atlantic Charter. After the service Minister Churchill made a radio broadcast explaining this choice:

"We sang 'Onward, Christian Soldiers' indeed, and I felt that this was no vain presumption, but that we had the right to feel that we are serving a cause for the sake of which a trumpet has sounded from on high. When I looked upon that densely packed congregation of fighting men of the same language, of the same faith, of the same fundamental laws, of the same ideals ... it swept across me that here was the only hope, but also the sure hope, of saving the world from measureless degradation."

What a profound statement from one of the most powerful leaders of the Allied cause. He explained what it would take to defeat such formidable opponents as Germany and Japan. Not once did he mention the overwhelming might of his navy vessels. He disregarded the power, speed, and finesse of the aircraft used in the Royal Air Force. In the eyes of Winston Churchill, the fighting men of the time were our ONLY hope for saving the world from total devastation and eventual slavery.

At the completion of the final bar of the song, Brother Jim dismissed the congregation to our 11am Sunday school classes. I attended the adult class with Del and all the other seniors for several years and never knew he had been a veteran. I had always enjoyed studying about World War II, but never had anyone who would share their first-hand experiences. Either they didn't want to rehash over painful memories, or they just didn't have good story telling skills.

I finally caught up to Del in the foyer of the church and asked where he had served. I was intrigued to find out what his experiences had been as a veteran of World War II. He replied, *"The Pacific."* The conversation continued with the mentioning of a type of ship I had never heard of before speaking with Del.

"I was a signalman on an LSM - Landing Ship Medium, (he added while carefully enunciating each word) *delivering tanks and flamethrower tankers to the shores of Iwo Jima."*

I listened intently as he spoke of Kamikazes, bombers, and typhoons. Just mentioning the suicide attacks and the typhoon gave me goose bumps. I hung on every word.

Introduction by the Author

"They came out of the clouds, all of the sudden, like hornets from a nest."...

"During that typhoon, I've never been more scared in my life"...

"He dropped three bombs just off our port side, and it shook the ship to the core"...

"I was on an L--S--M"...

These and other phrases rang through my mind for hours after we had spoken together. I still was a little fuzzy about the *"LSM"* thing. The emphasis on each letter of that three-letter acronym gave me an idea that my understanding of it was a matter of pride. Little did I know that I would learn just how important those modest two hundred-three foot ships and their crews would be to the cause of defeating the Japanese in the Pacific Theatre of Operations. Before the bell rang for the start of Sunday school, I had asked Del if he would allow me to write his recollections of the war. He cheerfully accepted, and we met on several occasions at his home and during lunches and dinners.

As soon as I could, I scoured the internet for any material and books about the topic of Landing Ship Mediums. I finally found two. One was a historical fiction based upon a veteran's experiences and the other was a historical biography of the crew of an LSM in the Pacific. I realized that there had been very little written about these greatly indispensable watercraft to the cause of defeating the Axis during World War II. The pressure was on to do this project justice.

This book was written in first person as though Del is telling it. Del's descriptions from his interviews would have been enough to tell the story. His skills in conveying an action or emotion were exemplary. I added the historical information when appropriate and the forensic details listed in the eight hundred page deck log that I had acquired from the National Archives. I had also received deck logs of other ships in the area of the LSM-143 during Operation Detachment (Battle of Iwo Jima) and used them in the book. These documents provide the story with dates, times, and confirmation of details. I owe so much gratitude to the folks at the National Archives for showing me unlimited patience and for sending the documents at *"flank"* speed. I will forever be in their debt.

Writing this book had been an experience that took me back in time. As I began to review the interviews and read the deck log, I was teleported to a different time as though I was living it. I WAS aboard the LSM-143 with every entry that I browsed from the logs. I spent hours dissecting the words of every page to get this book as accurate to time and detail as possible. I painstakingly placed the puzzle pieces that I received from the recorded interviews and the notes I had written as Del and I visited. Among each of these passages, I

Introduction by the Author

did my best to intertwine deck log information where it was needed. I hope readers will enjoy reading Del's account of his experiences as much as I enjoyed putting them to paper. It is my sincere wish that this work can be of historical value to anyone studying these wonderful amphibious vessels and their crews.

At the end of one of our interviews, Del made an insightful, matter-of-fact statement; *"So I had lots of experiences. They weren't all life or death experiences. But, I did have a lot of experiences."* After I completed this project, I wasn't too sure how safe things were for Del and the rest of the crew of the LSM-143 in the middle of the Pacific Ocean. Danger is relative. As the story continues, readers may have a different perspective as to just how safe Del and his fellow shipmates actually were against such a determined enemy.

I get the pleasure of talking to Del every Sunday at church. I'm proud to know him. He's a good Christian man who inspires me in many ways. As I listened to his stories, I know that he was, and is, a faithful man of God, wonderful husband and father to his five daughters. His childhood stories show me that it's OK to let go and take a chance; to go out and see new things. His reminiscences of battle that he shared with me continue that story of the adventurous boy that he left behind in Fountain, Michigan on that September day in 1943. This was a boy who volunteered at the age of seventeen to fight a war

General Quarters!

thousands of miles from home and give up his freedom to preserve ours. This was a war that saw our own soil being attacked. It was personal. Del mentions no regrets, only his pride in honor and duty to his country. It's an honor to know him, and call him my friend.

To Del – I will always consider you "family". You opened up your heart to me and shared your life and experiences. THAT can never be repaid. So, I will honor you with sharing this historical treasure with as many people as possible. Your story will live for generations. Thank you Del, and thank God for our friendship.

-Ray McCoy

TABLE OF CONTENTS

Chapter 1

THE BOY FROM FOUNTAIN, MICHIGAN

My father was born and raised in England. He had a younger brother, Robert, who came over a few years earlier to live in Quebec, Canada. My father came to visit his brother, and ended up staying. He stayed, that is, until he found a job as a laborer on a threshing machine where he would thresh beans, wheat, and so on. It wasn't long after that Uncle Robert moved back to England with his wife, and my father joined the Canadian Army. My father stuttered so badly that it took him too long to say "Garforth". He had a terrible time talking. He didn't talk much because he was so hard to understand. They misunderstood him when he was telling them that he was English. It took him too long to say "Garforth", so the Canadian army just called him "John English". That door was closed to me in checking my father's history. If I tried to trace him, I couldn't. There was no "Garforth" in the Canadian Army. There was a "John English"; that was my father.

With the end of World War I approaching, my father was scheduled to board the troop ship to go overseas when the Armistice of 1918 was declared. The ship never left the port in Quebec, and he was discharged just weeks later.

I don't know what brought him to Michigan except for the

fact that it is so close to Canada. He came to Fountain in 1921, and met Gladys Manchester. Somehow he met and married my mother, Gladys, later that same year. My father was a plumber by trade but he never became a master plumber. His boss even offered him journeyman papers and a regular route, but he never learned to drive a car so he missed out. Most of my father's work was in new construction, but he would also be sent on repair work as necessary. When I got older, my father took a job as a paver with a state road working crew.

It was so hard for him to talk, that I never learned much at all about my paternal family. I don't even know my grandfather or grandmother's name on his side. Of course my Grandpa and Grandma Garforth lived in England, and I never got to meet them. I had one sister, Leoma, two years older than

me. She died July of 2008, at 83, of some type of cancer.

I was born Delmor Dean Garforth in the small Great Lakes

town of Fountain, Michigan on August 31, 1926. Fountain is located in north-central Mason County in the Sherman Township, and was founded in 1882 as a station on the Pere Marquette Railroad. It was named by Nicholas J. Bockstanz from a spring he observed there, most likely near the north branch of Lincoln Creek, which flows through town. Fountain was organized as a village in 1913, and has survived the years primarily as a farming community and with a strong community spirit that reflects family, small business and hard work.

My family was poor Depression people, and we moved in with my Grandpa when times got tough. I was born in the same house, same bedroom, and same bed that my mother had been born in. I loved my Grandpa dearly, and worked hard on his farm growing and harvesting potatoes and various fruits.

My grandfather, Delbert Deville Manchester, was whom I was named after. I was proudly named Delmor Dean Garforth by my parents to stay with the "DD" thing. The first half of my name was for my grandfather (Delbert) and the second half came from my Aunt Ethal's infant son "Velmor" that died at birth. My name is not "Delmar", it's "Delmor". Well, of course, officially, it's "Delmar". At least that is what the doctor put on the birth certificate and that is what's on record. That name has been on all of my records ever since. It's on my school records, medical records, and it was on the muster roll while I was in the Navy. Evidently, the doctor had never heard of the name "Delmor". Well, rather than fight it, I just went with it. However, my family always called me "Delmor" regardless. Most people I know now just call me "Del".

My grandpa was a 'Jack-of-all-trades'. As far as I was concerned, my grandpa could do anything. He was a farmer, carpenter, plumber, and just everything. My grandpa's family was from New York State. They were pioneers to the town of

D.D. Manchester Office & Coal Shed 1915

Fountain when they moved there in the late 1800's. When he got to Fountain, he started out as a farmer. By 1910 he had opened a successful coal distribution business like the one he had started in New York. In 1919, he had to sell the business and begin work for a motor company as a mechanic. Six years later, he took a job as a carpenter with a local building company. By the time I had gotten old enough to remember, my grandpa was back into farming. My grandpa had tried everything and that's what made him so versatile. I admired my grandpa so much that I wanted to be just like him. I watched everything that he did with care so that I could emulate every move. He would whistle while he worked, so I would try really hard to mimic his sound. I sounded more like a deflating bicycle tire than a songbird. But, I was a "big guy" like Grandpa.

For a couple of years I had a bummed childhood physically. At the age of nine, I had woken up one winter morning with a sore throat, fever, and achy joints. My mother allowed me to stay home from school that day to rest and try to recover. But, as the day progressed, I just got worse. My muscles all over my body began to ache. My mom and dad didn't worry a whole lot until the next day when my hands and feet started jerking just the slightest little bit at first. Then, by day's end, I couldn't even walk without falling down, or I would drop something that I was trying to carry. They took me to the doctor who informed us that I had contracted Rheumatic Fever and the condition that sometimes accompanies the disease: Chorea.

This condition is commonly known as Saint Vitus Dance, and is so named after Saint Vitus who was the Christian patron saint of dancers. It causes the person to shake uncontrollably. It is best characterized by rapid, uncoordinated jerking movements primarily affecting the face, hands, and feet. When one walks, it actually looks as though that person is dancing a very graceful tango except without control of any of the moves. Chorea is derived from the Greek word "choreia" which means "to dance". The root word is also used in the word "choreography" which is the development of dance moves. The movements cease during sleep, and the disease will run its course after several months.

Even though my father wouldn't say much, he was a dear, sweet, and gentle man. He would rub my back and my legs to help alleviate the pain of my condition. Every time I would feel pain, he would do everything he could to make it better. Despite all of my father's efforts, this condition finally caused me to spend my 10th birthday in the hospital.

Nevertheless, I was always able to retain my adventurous side. The disease had run its course after a few weeks, and I was getting restless in that hospital room. The shaking and the soreness had all but subsided. I just had a small twinge here and there, but nothing that kept me from doing the things that I had longed to do for months. Suffering from this crazy disease is like being a prisoner in one's own body. The arm is supposed to do this, and it does that. The person tries to walk in one direction, and the legs travel to the other. It is especially hard for a kid that has been used to going crazy outside climbing trees and swimming in Lake Michigan. I was finally able to break out of that prison in which my body had me locked.

There was a reporter for the local paper, the Ludington Daily News, whom my dad had asked to pick me up from the hospital in Ann Arbor. We took off for home in his brand new 1936 Chevrolet. He took me as far as Ludington, and dropped me off at the jail. Well, the sheriff put me in a cell where I was told that I could spend the night. I had a soda on the ride to the jail, and was wandering the corridors looking for a restroom. I was spotted by the Sheriff's wife who was appalled at the living quarters her husband had allotted me. They had an apartment right in the jail. She was a motherly type and took me under her wing. Well, she jumped her husband for putting me in a cell, and she took me into their apartment to spend the night. So, the next morning, she fed me breakfast. I'm not sure what excuse I made, but I walked out of there. Well, I didn't just walk; I ran! I ran clear to what they call *"the 4th Ward"*. I took advantage of my new found freedom, and it was exhilarating. I was full of vigor. I was alive again. Once again, I was bulletproof.

The town of Ludington was strung out. I had ran about five or six miles to where I ended up. There was a refinery there where a family friend named Fred Hansen worked. I knew Fred came to work that day so I hung around a while. I plopped myself up onto the drink cooler that was sitting on the porch of the main office. Sure enough, just after day break, he shows up in his big flatbed 1929 Ford truck.

"Del is that you? Boy, you're growin' like a weed. What are you doing this far from home?"

"I busted out of the hospital, and I want to go home."

"Well, I'm making a delivery in Scottville. You can tag along if you want. I can take you as far as the courthouse, and you can hitch a ride from there."

"That's swell Mr. Hansen! Thanks!"

"Here's a nickel. Get you a drink out of that cooler you were sitting on and hop in."

He chucked the nickel in a coin-toss fashion. I caught it and ran back up to the porch, dropped in the nickel, and pulled out the soda. Like a real professional, I flicked the lid off in one quick motion of the opener bolted to the front of the cooler. About as quick as you could hear the hiss from the carbonation, I had that curvy glass bottle bottoms-up. I mean I was thirsty by the time Mr. Hansen got there. I'm sure that his fatherly intuition told him so. I jumped on the running board of his truck and heaved on the handle. The door bounced open on its hinges as I leapt to the seat. I reached over, grabbed the handle, and leaned back with my upper body to shut that big heavy door. Mr. Hansen pushed the stick into first gear and gunned the engine. With a lurch, I was heading home. I rolled the window down and off we went. It was great to be on the road again. I stuck my head out the window like a dog and felt the cool breeze. It just refreshed my soul.

Fred weaved the old Ford around the road up to the courthouse and dropped me off at the front door. I could tell he was concerned for me, but he had to get to his deliveries.

"Are you gonna be alright, Del?"

"I'll be fine, Mr. Hansen. Someone will be along in a minute to get me. Thanks for the lift!"

I didn't tell Mr. Hansen that I had no one in particular picking me up so that he wouldn't feel obligated to stick around. Either way, one of my friends came along and picked me up. He didn't have enough room in the car for me, so I rode five miles standing on the running board and hanging onto the door post. When he dropped me off at home, I walked into the laundry room where my mother was. Anyway, my mother almost passed out. She thought I was still in the hospital, in Ann Arbor, more than 300 miles away. I was old before my time. I felt that I could handle traveling by myself. I wouldn't

Del, age 16, on the beach of Lake Michigan

try the same thing today if I was a ten year old boy. But, back in those days, we didn't worry about it. Luckily, I grew out of my shaky condition before long, but I think it left me with a nervous disposition.

***

All my life, I had been very fond of the tranquil, picturesque beaches of Lake Michigan. Countless days were spent on these beaches. I was so partial to Lake Michigan beaches. They had some beautiful beaches. I didn't have any wheels; my little town was 20 miles inland from Ludington. Anytime we went to the beach, it was a treat for my sister and me. We would go after my Grandpa took care of his work for the day. There was a breakwater that went way out, and there was a lighthouse on the end. The little lighthouse near Ludington was a white, wooden structure that was built in 1870, and displayed a fixed red light using a fifth-order Fresnel lens. That little lighthouse was really a thing of beauty. Actually, I don't think I have ever seen a lighthouse that wasn't beautiful especially the ones we saw on the way home from the war.

It was quite a trick just to walk out to the breakwater because it would throw up a bunch of waves. Lake Michigan was all sandy bottom. There was a spot where some of us guys liked to swim. We would throw coins or something and let them sink, and then dive for them in 20 feet of water. It was the best of times!

We did a lot of fishing, and fishing was good in Lake Michigan. There was a small bait shop at the base of the breakwater that sold minnows and whatever else we needed. We bought our minnows right there and went fishing. We would run down to the edge of the water and throw our lines in. The view across the expansive lake was completely breathtaking, and the breeze off the lake was absolutely intoxicating. It was as much a pleasure to watch the water as it was to fish. However, I loved fresh caught perch and blue gills. I wasn't much for big fish, and northern pike had too many bones. Whatever fish that I caught that day, I took it home, cleaned it, and took it in to my momma. She would bread it really nice with flour. She would boil some crunchy, sweet corn on the cob and some green beans from Grandpa's garden. Then, we would all sit down and devour the whole lot. My mouth is watering right now just thinking about the fresh water perch and blue gill.

***

I got my driver's license at the age of fourteen, and it had to be pretty close to my birthday. It was established that everyone could get their first license at age fourteen. There was no driver's training or anything like that. We lived out in the country and we learned to drive at a very early age. There was no police out there. Now, my friend George who was about three years older than me let me drive his dad's Model T. He was my pal and my next door neighbor. Anytime he could get his dad's car, he would come get me. We would just go for a ride, and he would let me drive. I actually learned to drive while riding around with my pal George and my grandpa. I took it easy with his Dad's old "Tin Lizzie" at first until

George gouged me to open it up.

"For Pete's sakes Del, floor it!"

Without any hesitation, I pulled it back into second and floored the old car. It wasn't like it squealed the tires or anything, but we certainly threw up the dust. It was fun for a fourteen year old. We weaved around the curves and the old car would respond by squeaking and swaying with each turn of the wheel. George would reach over and blow the horn with approval. There weren't any seatbelt laws, so we just bounced and slid on that old bench seat banging shoulder to shoulder at every twist in the road. It was a stiff old car to drive, but we had a ball. We would stop at the gas station in Scottville, and George would check the oil while I pumped fifty cents worth of gas into the tank. That was enough for about five gallons. Both of us would get a cherry soda out of the cooler for five cents and guzzle it down. Then, it was back in the saddle to tear up the roads again.

Our county seat was Ludington, right on Lake Michigan. That was our shopping center, and maybe twice a year we would get into Ludington. My granddad would let me drive but not down the highway. He would only let me drive on the secondary roads. I hopped in the driver's seat, and we would zigzag until we got to Highway 10 on the outskirts of Ludington. Then, I would stop, park, and let my Grandpa take over from there.

Just after my fourteenth birthday, we took the same back

roads to Ludington to get my license. When I got to the crossroads of Highway 10 to let my Grandpa take over, he said,

"No. That's OK. You can drive now. Go on your way to get your license."

Back before the war, you filled out a license every year. There was no such thing as getting a license for three or four years. You had to take this written test standing at the counter of the police department. Every year, they would ask if you could read the bottom line of the eye test. I would say,

"Sure. P-L-O-T-E."

I knew the chart from the year before. I didn't even have to look up. After a few times, the clerk would get wise and say,

"OK. Read the next to bottom row…backwards."

It's a good thing that I could see better back then.

Every boy has these stages in their lives where they can't wait to grow up and be a man. Then, when we get older, we wish for the opposite. When I got my license, it was the first time in my life that I felt like a man. There would be several other times that I felt I had to prove myself. The times when I told my parents, *"See I can do this."* I would find out that my next step was coming just around the corner in the form of a two hundred three foot water borne vessel. This ship would be my home for almost two years on the largest body of water on earth.

Chapter 2

RETRIBUTION

November 1941: From the northern most of the main Japanese islands, six Japanese aircraft carriers were brought to full strength to go to war with the United States and the British Empire. Japan was going to war because she had been unable to find no other way to relieve the economic sanctions which the United States has placed against her. From the oil of the Dutch East Indies to the rubber of Sumatra and Burma, and for the free hand in the conquest of China, Japan felt that it had no choice but to go to war.

In Europe, France and Holland have fallen, England was all but defeated, and Russia had been invaded by the Germans. All of the restraining powers but one were incapable of stopping Japan in their conquest of needed raw materials and expansionism.

Under the greatest secrecy, Vice Admiral Chuichi Nagumo, an experienced, cautious officer, took his ships to sea on 26 November 1941; with orders to abort the mission if he was discovered, or should diplomacy work come to an agreement. The Japanese fleet began to steam toward the Hawaiian Islands and the island of Oahu. Its mission was to destroy the US

General Quarters!

Pacific Fleet with one crippling surprise attack. All six of Japan's first-line aircraft carriers, *Akagi, Kaga, Soryu, Hiryu, Shokaku* and *Zuikaku*, were assigned to the mission. With over four hundred twenty embarked planes, these ships constituted by far the most powerful carrier task force ever assembled. Nagumo's Pearl Harbor Striking Force also included fast battleships, cruisers and destroyers, with auxiliary oilers to fuel the ships during their passage across the Pacific. An Advance Expeditionary Force of large submarines, five of them carrying midget submarines, were sent to scout around Hawaii, dispatch the midgets into Pearl Harbor to attack ships there, and torpedo American warships that might escape to sea.

November 27, 1941: A message was received in code at Pearl Harbor from the Chief of Naval Operations in Washington, DC to the office of the Commander of the United States Pacific Fleet. *"This dispatch is to be considered a war warning. Diplomatic negotiations with Japan have ceased and an aggressive move by Japan is expected in the next few days. Execute appropriate defensive maneuvers."*

A Japanese secret message was intercepted and later decoded in Washington which came from the Japanese office in Tokyo to the Japanese Consulate in Hawaii. *"Strictly secret. Please investigate comprehensively the American fleet bases in the neighborhood of the Hawaiian military reservation."*

December 2, 1941: The American Navy reported that it

had lost track of the Japanese aircraft carriers Divisions 1 and 2. The American intelligence assumed that the fleet was near home waters on maneuvers.

December 5, 1941: With diplomatic prospects firmly at an end, Nagumo received a message from Admiral Isoroku Yamamoto that read, *"Climb Mount Niitaka."* Its meaning: *"Proceed with attack"*. Yamamoto was inspired by a fictional account of a possible war with Japan and the United States titled *"The Great Pacific War: A History of the American-Japanese Campaign of 1931-33"*. Written sixteen years before the attack on Pearl Harbor by Hector Bywater, it gave a detailed blow by blow account of what could happen if these two powers went to war in the Pacific. At the time the novel was written, the US Fleet was stationed in a naval harbor in the Philippines. Nevertheless, Yamamoto used this book written by a British author as inspiration in his planning for the attack on the US Navy fleet at Pearl Harbor.

Midnight, December 6, 1941: The American Military received a report that the Japanese consulate was burning papers under the cover of night. No steps were taken by the US military.

Between the times of 0042 until 0333, December 7, 1941: Near Oahu's southern shore, the five midget submarines were cast from their "mother" subs at different points around the harbor entrance. The mother subs were ordered to remain in the area for later re-docking of the midget subs after the attack.

0600 hours: The Japanese strike force was two hundred miles north of Pearl Harbor. The carriers were brought to full speed and turned twenty degrees to starboard in order to launch the planes fully into the wind. There were one hundred thirty-five dive bombers, forty torpedo bombers, one hundred four high level bombers, and eighty-one fighter escorts. To double check their navigation, the Japanese flyers tuned in the American radio station on Oahu. The station unknowingly served as a radio beacon that guided the Japanese attackers towards Pearl Harbor.

0700 hours: The anti-torpedo net protecting the American fleet at Pearl was unexplainably left open.

0712 hours: A decoded message from the American destroyer, USS Ward (DD-139), announced that it had fired upon a Japanese midget submarine in the harbor. These were the first shots fired in combat during World War II. There was no decisive action taken, and the message was pending confirmation.

0717 hours: An American private using an experimental radar set, telephoned that he had picked up an unknown flight of fifty planes heading south toward Pearl Harbor. His commander received the report, and disregarded the mass of aircraft as "friendly".

0755 hours: The first wave of Japanese planes attacked the

American airfield to prevent a counter attack.

0757 hours: The major strike against the primary target began on battleship row; the backbone of the Pacific Fleet.

In less than two hours, seven of the eight battleships were either sunk or seriously damaged. The events at Pearl Harbor erase America's misconception and debate over "isolationism".

1230 hours, December 8, 1941: The United States of America now spoke with one voice as President Franklin D. Roosevelt announced over every radio in America. At 12:30 local time in Washington DC the speech was delivered in front of the Joint Session of Congress. The legendary *"Infamy"* speech orated so eloquently by Franklin Delano Roosevelt began:

"Vice President, Mr Speaker, members of the Senate, and the House of Representatives: Yesterday, December 7, 1941, a date which will live in infamy. The United States of America was suddenly and deliberately attacked by naval and air forces of the Empire of Japan."

Within an hour of the close of that seven minute speech, Congress passed a formal declaration of war against Japan which officially catapulted the United States into World War II.

The attack on Pearl Harbor was a tactical success that greatly reduced America's naval capabilities in the Pacific Theatre of Operations on that seventh day of December in

1941. But, as the months wore on, the Japanese realized that it was a strategic failure. The Japanese realized that they had only *"awakened a sleeping giant and filled him with resolve."* That line comes from Isoroku Yamamoto's final statement in the movie *Tora! Tora! Tora!* It has never been verified that he ever actually said those words, but we do know that after the attack, it was a true statement. The attack unified the citizens of the country, giving us the singular purpose of defeating the aggressor. Women and men alike left their homes and regular jobs to work in converted automobile factories where they riveted together more warships to replace the ones lost at Pearl. Our boys were lining up at the recruiting offices to join the fight on land, air, and sea. Anywhere the enemy could hide, we would find them; even on something as expansive as the Pacific Ocean.

***

I was fifteen years old on December 7th, 1941 when my family and I sat around the radio to witness the news of the surprise attack. Without a care in the world, we were listening to the radio on that Sunday afternoon just after church and a wonderful meal that my mom had prepared. It was a time that we all enjoyed sitting in the living room with full bellies listening the shows. The static-filled sound of the song *"A Little Jive is Good For You"* by Martha Tilton was resonating over the monotone speaker from our radio. The announcer broke the melody at mid-stream with the history making statement:

"We interrupt this program to bring you a special news

bulletin. The Japanese have attacked Pearl Harbor, Hawaii by air; President Roosevelt has just announced. The attack was made on all naval and military activities on the principal island of Oahu."

We just couldn't believe what we were hearing. Over the past several months, we had been reassured by the Japanese that we were their ally and there would continue to be peace between our nations. The next morning, the following excerpt from FDR's speech linger fresh in my mind.

"No matter how long it may take us to overcome this premeditated invasion, the American people in their righteous might will win through to absolute victory! ...We will gain the inevitable triumph; so help us God!"

General Quarters!

My grandpa always read through the paper, and I remember looking over his shoulder as he read the headline on Monday morning: *U.S. DECLARES WAR ON JAP EMPIRE*

THE LUDINGTON DAILY NEWS

U. S. DECLARES WAR ON JAP EMPIRE TODAY

Jap Bombs Shatter Peace

President Roosevelt Speaks; Reveals U.S. Has Lost Two Warships in Sunday's Attack

TODAY. We read the article still numb from the news we had heard on the radio.

Elsewhere, were advertisements of all kinds for Christmas gifts for your wife or toys for the kids. Morris Five and Dime had games, toys, candies, and novelties that cost from five to up to fifty cents. It sounded like a great deal for a tight budget like our family. Baltzer's Auto had the "big and roomy" 1942 Studebaker Champion for eight hundred ten dollars off the lot. It was made of the *"finest materials and craftsmanship"* and got *"remarkable gas and oil mileage"*. At the Star Theatre in Scottville, *"Dive Bomber"* starring Errol Flynn and Fred

Retribution

MacMurray was playing for eleven cents for kids and twenty-five cents for adults. This, by the way, was a pretty good flick showcasing actual footage of the Vought Vindicator and the US Navy. I thought it was rather ironic that a dive bomber movie was playing at the theater.

We had gone to the Star Theater in Scottville to see that movie that weekend. The movie was perfect timing to really motivate our young minds into absolutely hating the Japanese. All movies from that point until the end of the war were preempted by a two or three-minute patriotic newsreel. The speaker narrated

the action with stark descriptions of what we were witnessing on the big screen:

"The cowardly Japanese attack was relentless. As wave

after wave of carrier-based aircraft swarmed down on our unsuspecting Pacific fleet. Huge columns of dense black smoke billow up and block out the sun. Eight battleships are sunk or badly damaged. Many other ships are crippled by bombs and torpedoes. Thousands of American sailors, soldiers, and Marines are killed or wounded."

The newsreel ends with a rehashing of President Roosevelts speech introduction:

"Yesterday, December 7th, 1941, a date which will live in infamy..."

I remember leaving the theater wanting to sign up right then and there. I was only fifteen at the time, so I knew that it was an impossible notion. I would have to wait and watch on the sidelines while I read about the action in the newspaper.

Christmas was usually an exciting time of year, but it was hard to fully enjoy the cheery advertisements for the news of war. A sub-article in the paper about the aerial attack on the Philippine Islands was also front-page news. I knew my geography pretty well as a fifteen year old and reasoned just how close the Japs were to our west coast. If they could get their planes to Hawaii, California was next. In my imagination, I figured that the Japs had aircraft carriers just like the one they had pictured in the newspaper that morning heading for our coast.

I recall the goose bumps that overtook my body from hearing Roosevelt's speech. I remember feeling that we had to gain retribution. I remember saying, *"We have to get back at those Dirty Japs"*. I was ready for some action when I became fifteen. I had made a foolish statement once, *"I hope the war doesn't end too soon because I want to fight them Japs!"* I would get my chance two years after that day of "infamy".

Over the next couple of years, I kept myself busy on my Grandpa's farm helping him plant and harvest the crops. Every time there was a paper at the house, he would read to us and I would read along. I was living out the stories that we would read about. I had imagined where the boys who were already old enough to go off to war were sent to fight. I wondered if they had been killed, or how many Japs or Germans they had killed. I couldn't wait to hear what was happening next and

how our boys were fairing. The Ludington Daily News was full of heroic stories of "Nipponese" defeats at Midway Island, Guadalcanal, Goodenough, Russell Islands, Woodlark,

General Quarters!

Kiriwina, Rendova, Nassau Bay, New Georgia, Vella Lavella, and the list went on and on. I was a little curious and a whole lot bored. So, I had a school book with maps that I would scan through and follow precisely the location of these battles. I don't really remember exactly, but I think it must have been a Geography or History book of some kind. I tried to imagine what it would be like to be there. I imagined just how brave I knew I would be fighting the Japs. I would be fearlessly pushing them back into the Pacific. It is absolutely blissful being fifteen years old. You think you know everything about the world and how to handle yourself. You definitely know more about life than your parents. That's why they send young men to war. We were young and foolish at that age. We were bulletproof. It doesn't take too many years to learn differently. Sometimes it just takes a calm wind to steer you in the right direction. But, most of the time it takes a good kick in the pants. That's what war does to a young man. It is a GENUINE reality check.

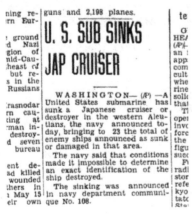

News in August of 1942 was speaking of submarines, dive bombers, and naval destroyers sinking Jap ships just off the Aleutian Islands. In the August 19th edition, we had sunk twenty-three enemy ships in that conflict alone. This was getting way too close to home. All the "Nips" had to do was to head south, down the coast, and they would be on our mainland. These American

victories were welcoming news. I was sixteen when we read of the Japanese evacuation from Guadalcanal and we had kept the Japs from cutting off our supply routes to and taking over Australia. In six months I would be seventeen and old enough to join the fight with my parents' consent. I was biting at the bit. I was tired of just reading about the war. I was ready to go.

Not wanting to have anything to do with foxholes, I joined the US Navy at the age of seventeen with my parents' permission. My mother grew tired of my badgering so she grabbed the paper from my hand. She leaned over the paper on the kitchen table and signed on the parental consent line. With a sorrowful look on her face, she held it out to me. *"Now, go."*

General Quarters!

I gingerly took the paper from my mom as I looked into her sad eyes. She had heard news of too many mothers losing their young boys. When I got out the kitchen door, I literally ran the permission papers down to the Navy recruiting office and proudly handed them to the guy at the desk. He checked my age and my Mom's signature and began my induction process.

I never regretted the choice because I watched so many

men killed during the battle of Iwo Jima. I felt that compared to the Marines and other soldiers who had to fight hand-to-hand combat, I had it made. I always had a hot meal; no C-rations or K-rations.

Retribution

In September 1943, scores of new recruits and I exited the train at the Great Lakes Naval Training Station in Great Lakes, Illinois. In single file, we grabbed the rail and stepped down the steep steps to the ground of the base for the first time. A group of sailors walked by pointing at us "*newbies*":

"New birds!"

"You'll be sorry!"

"Wait until the barber gets ahold of ya, Mac!"

"They've got the needles sharpened for ya Fella!"

An officer met us at the terminal and directed us to follow him:

"Alright men, bring all your gear, form in threes!"

The officer introduced himself and began to fill us in on the details of our wonderful experience we were about to embark upon. He continued in his best southern accent.

"Welcome to Great Lakes Naval Base! You people are not citizens anymore and you sure as heck ain't sailors. You are nothing. You are dog turds. But, your butts are mine. Do you hear me? Mine! Now, for the next six weeks, I will provide you with everything you need. I will personally make sure that you get some REAL stylish clothing. My personal hair stylist will give you an ever so light trim over your ears. I will also make sure that you get a REAL comfortable bed and, by Golly, I will

teach you how to make that darn thing. After a night of uninterrupted sleep, I will quietly come into your barracks and very tenderly wake you up. I will personally make sure that our very own chef serves you a hot, nourishing international cuisine for breakfast. From there, I will take you to the dispensary where the most beautiful nurse in the whole U S of A will tell you to drop your drawers and stick a four inch needle into every soft spot on your body including your bee-hind! Now, don't that sound like lots of fun? It is! You and me are going to have loads of fun! Follow me! Let's go!"

The officer marched us from the train station and down the road to the chain-linked main gate. We were paraded down by a group of marching sailors that we thought were *"old salts"*. But, they were no more than a couple of weeks ahead of us. It looked kind of funny seeing sailors march with guns. I guess I had envisioned the whole *"Navy"* thing to be just boats and sea spray. I pictured it as swabbing the deck, battening down hatches, and weighing the anchor. The latter is one of the things I had to unlearn from watching naval movies as a kid. I had always thought that the phrase was *"anchor's away"*. This was of the innocent reckoning that the anchor was "away" and plunging into the water. In fact, we learned it was *"anchors aweigh"* meaning that all anchors have been *"weighed"* or raised. We also tried to figure out why the Navy insisted that we call one side of the ship *"port"* and the other *"starboard"*. It goes right along with why they insist on calling everything you can possibly walk on *"the deck"*. If you have to relieve yourself, you enter something that is called the *"head"*. You eat in the *"galley"*. Fortunately, *"walking the plank"* is reserved for pirates.

This place would be referred to by most of the guys after a while as *"Great Mistakes"*. It was the name sailors gave the Great Lakes training facilities when we realized that we could have been at the San Diego facility enjoying much better weather. I was used to the weather. I grew up on Lake Michigan, and had been used to the cold. The Great Lakes facility was located due north of Chicago and in a southwest direction across the lake from Ludington and Fountain. I felt more at home there than anyone. I had spent my entire young life on that lake. Even though the shore was alien to me, the waters weren't.

The officer directed us into the large meeting building that served as our movie house when we had some leisure time.

"Boys! This here is the theater. The only thing missing is the popcorn and that sweet young girl that you left back home. But don't worry; your next door neighbor's boy will take care of her while you are here with me. Enjoy the film."

This time we got to watch the orientation film for boots. The gung ho music bellowed from the speakers that sounded like an old Popeye cartoon. It was an induction film that went through the basics of terms and things that we would encounter on our first few days there. Little did I know that the film left out some very important details about some of the things I wasn't used to as a boy in Michigan.

We were introduced to our barracks that first night. The walls were labeled like a ship. The back of the room was the "*STERN*", the front was the "*BOW*", and the bathroom was labeled the "*CREWS' HEAD*". The first night seemed like living in a station waiting room. Our beds were stacked in there like shoe boxes, and it was just one huge rectangular room. I didn't get a whole lot of sleep that first night. Some guy was snoring a couple of bunks down, and the noxious fumes from their backsides were almost unbearable. I just had to learn to give that right back. I remember looking around and thinking, "*I don't know any of these jerks. How am I gonna live with these people that I don't even know?*" I'm sure they were thinking the same thing about having to live with perfect strangers even though there was nothing perfect about any of us. All that went through my mind all night was what was going to happen next. We had heard the horror stories from the guys who had been there a while. I tried to get all that out of my mind, but I had a heck of a time getting that smell out of my nose.

The second day, the officer lined us up in threes again and

marched us down to the medical aid building. As soon as we got packed into the reception room, the sailor up front on the intercom announced:

"Remove all civilian clothing for shipment home."

"Print all shipping labels carefully."

So we began taking off every stitch of clothes we had on. I mean we stripped all the way down to the buff. I looked around and there was nothing in that room to put on in the place of what I was taking off. I knew right then that they were going to parade us around a while like this, in our birthday suits. There is nothing more humbling or more demeaning than to be completely bare in front of scores of other guys. Even though the air was perfectly warm when we entered the room, my exposed skin shivered as I tried to hide the feeling. Other guys walked around the room passing out flat pieces of cardboard that I quickly folded out into a box. I folded my shirt, pants, and jacket as neatly as I could and placed them into the box first. Then, I laid the socks and underwear that I took off on top. I tried not to look down or act like I was looking at anyone so they wouldn't think I was *"funny"*. I just concentrated on writing out the label as neatly as I could with my home address in Fountain.

Then after I stood shivering in the nude in a large room with hundreds of other men, a Navy supply clerk tossed at me the uniforms and *"skivvies"* I would wear during my period of enlistment. *"Skivvies"* is Navy slang for underwear. They piled uniforms on my arms, with little attention to size, that every recruit learned to wear, not always the proper way at first. The only thing we were allowed to wear at that time was the skivvies.

After we got on our skivvies, we were given one of the scores of vaccinations the Navy deemed necessary during our six week period in boot camp. It wasn't any big deal to me, but a few guys would pass out and hit the floor before one of the corpsmen could catch them. Most of them stung like crazy, but I never passed out. One guy went completely face first and blood just gushed everywhere from his nose. I'm pretty confident that he broke his nose. The nurse and an orderly picked him up and placed him on one of the beds and began first aid.

As the day went along, we just learned to grit our teeth and take it on whatever area of the body that was necessary. It seemed like that was every square inch of our butt cheeks and each arm. They continued to examine each of us. I was taken to x-ray, the dentist, optometrist, and my blood pressure and pulse were all taken. I knew that I was healthy as a horse. I had been running around northeastern Michigan all of my young life and swimming the Great Lakes. I could dive fifteen feet down and swim for hundreds of yards out to the middle of Lake Michigan and back. I was in as good of shape as any athlete; as good as anyone there. I passed all of their tests with flying colors.

We still clung to what little bit of individuality that we possessed; our glorious haircuts. Many of us had spent hard earned money every so often at the barber shop at home with a skilled barber who had honed his craft over years of sculpting just the right style. It was usually the style of the times. They weren't fancy, mind you. But, it gave us some since of eccentricity. I remember telling the barber back home, *"Cecil, take a little off the sides, and part it to the right. Throw in a little witch-hazel while you're at it. I want the works."*

However, that aspect of our existence was about to run its course in just a few steps to the barber shop. Well, it couldn't really be called a barber shop. It was a row of chairs with men standing in waiting behind each with an electric razor in hand. These men didn't have to have a skill in the least at cosmetology. All they had to do was have good enough eyesight to see our heads, raise one arm, and run the blades about six good times around our melons until the hair fell to the deck-notice I didn't say *"floor"*. We no longer had need for a comb or brush. All we needed was a good bar of soap and some water to rub it into our clean, bristly scalp. On top of that, there was no witch-hazel.

By this time, we all looked almost identical. Our moms would have barely recognized us. We were all the same. We were no longer individuals. We were now "*Navy*". We could no longer be identified as city boys, country boys, or farm boys. We would be trained to be one, cohesive unit. We were to become scores of cylinders firing one engine. It was teamwork to the nth degree. Navy boot camp was designed to transform an individual from a soft civilian to a rugged, fighting seaman.

The Navy then gave us our sleeping gear. In the tradition of the old navy, they issued a hammock with a mattress, two mattress covers affectionately referred to as "*fart sacks*", one pillow, two pillow covers, and two blankets. The "*boot*" needed a place to store these items, so one of the first items issued to him was his sea bag.

This cylindrical canvas sack of 26" x 36" had grommets on top through which I wove a line to use as a draw string to close the bag and to hang it from a rack-Notice that I didn't say "*bed*". As with everything else I got, I stenciled my name on the side of the bag. This bag is a sailor's possession and his alone. It was his absolute and exclusive identity as an individual among the throng of other men. When traveling, a sailor rolled his mattress and sleeping gear inside the hammock which he then wrapped around and secured to his sea bag. He slung the pack up on a shoulder and marched off with all he owned. Before rolling his mattress, however, a sailor laid out his bedding items on the flattened mattress in a specific order according to regulations.

The order was not haphazard. It came from much experience and resulted in a compact package when rolled. Sailors did not just stuff their clothing into their sea bag. It had to be prepared first according to regulations and then inserted in a particular order. This procedure insured first that the clothing would take up a minimum of space so it would all fit in the sea bag. Secondly, by rolling items and tying them they tended to have fewer wrinkles when unrolled. The manner in which a Boot's clothing was prepared was not only regulation, but practical.

Then all boots were issued *The Bluejacket's Manual* which the Navy referred to as the "*sailor's bible*". This book was first issued to sailors in 1902 and has gone through twenty-four editions. During World War II, editions ten, eleven, or twelve were issued to sailors from 1940 to 1945. My copy of the manual was the eleventh edition which was issued to sailors from 1943 to 1944. This book contained all the instructions the boot would need to know to become a sailor and handle himself as such. Phrases like:

"Up and at 'em!"

"Drop 'em and grab 'em!"

"Scrub down that deck!"

"Move it Boot! Now! I ain't your mommy asking you! I'm

telling you!"

These and other commands the Chief Petty Officer assigned to a boot company shouted. These commands were issued mostly in the middle of the night after a hard, tiring, long, ten-hour day of marching, calisthenics, scrubbing clothes, rifle-over-your-head drills, pulling oars in a boat, loading heavy shells in a five inch gun, and other training activities. The obvious reason for harassing the boots was to get them accustomed to discipline, to respond to disagreeable orders, to function with little sleep, and probably to give the Chief his kicks. Either way, it worked. Our navy was the best on any ocean, and the US sailor was the reason.

World War II Navy Boot Camps ground out thousands of sailors well enough trained to go aboard ships and win the war. Boot Camp training lasted about six weeks plus or minus a couple depending on the Navy's need at the moment for men in the fleet. Finally, the moment came; the graduating companies fell in for a parade and pass in review. Then the commander declared the Boots had finished their training and would get leave to go home and display their uniforms with pride.

When a Boot graduated from Boot Camp he became a new sailor. I had my mattress rolled and my sea bag full. Then I formed the rolled mattress around the sea bag and restrained it with a line. Proudly, with a laboring grunt, I swung it up and balanced it on my shoulder. At that moment I marched off to my first leave and my next assignment, Signal School. Now I no longer felt or thought like a boot. I was a sailor, and would start my journey now with the Navy.

***

My training included "Signal School" which involved flagging and spotlight operation. In the U.S. Navy, "Signalman" was a naval rate (job type) combining both visual short-range communications, and advanced lookout skills. While there was certainly a signalman rating before World War II, the Signalman rating is one of the oldest in the Navy. Signalmen were identified by the symbol of two crossed semaphore flags on the right sleeve of the uniform integrated with their rank insignia. The nickname around every ship for a signalman was *"skivvy waver"*. I imagine that someone down the line figured that it looked like we were waving our underwear around. I can't remember ever putting my underwear on the end of a stick though. Anyway, when you are pinned with a nickname, it's just better to go with it.

Signalmen were responsible for transmitting, receiving, encoding, decoding, and distributing messages obtained via the visual transmission systems of semaphore, visual Morse code (flashing light), and flag hoist signaling.

The Signalman rate played a highly significant role in both

ship to ship and ship to shore communications. Visual signals were used to maneuver ships in formation, to transmit emergency signals, tactical signals and routine communications.

Semaphore was a rapid and secure means of transmitting visual messages. It made use of two hand flags attached to staffs about twenty-two inches long. That increased range of visibility. Semaphore could be used to send messages to several addresses at one time if they were positioned properly; because of its speed, it was better adapted for long messages. Semaphore and flashing light could be used interchangeably. Semaphore was much faster and generally more secure than flashing light for short-distance transmission in clear daylight. Care had to be exercised in selecting a good background from which to send a semaphore message. The better the background behind the signalman, the greater the signaling distance.

Flashing light was used daily on the signal bridge. To become a searchlight operator, a Signalman must be efficient in Morse code. He must be knowledgeable in all procedures when communicating via flashing light. Searchlight operators must be able to energize equipment and to spot any malfunctions. Not only was the light used for communications, it was also utilized during nighttime loading and unloading of cargo into the ship's well deck.

Working with flags was an integral part of the Signalman's job. Flags were used to send messages and tactical signals during daylight, to identify a ship's nationality, and, on occasion, to indicate the seniority of an officer or civil official on board.

General Quarters!

Signalmen were also recognized as *"professional look-outs"* and were well versed at identifying all types of surface ships, submarines when surfaced, and aircraft. The

signalman's job was an outside profession. Their duty station was always posted on the highest part of the ship, generally very near or on top of the ships bridge, which gave them the best visual advantage. The very nature of the job made the signalman a natural born witness to events. If it involved operations, rescues, weather events or anything that happened on the exterior of the ship, chances are that a signalman saw what happened. On every ship, the signalman had an extremely important job. Even with good radar, a good lookout was one of the OOD's (*Officer on Deck*) most valuable sources of information. A signalman's duties by nature required keeping a sharp lookout. As a matter of pride, the signalman should be the first to sight and identify objects. An expert lookout had to be plenty sharp on a lot of things. Not only did lookouts have to sight and identify objects, they had to report them correctly, using relative bearings, distances, target angles, and in the case of aircraft, position angles.

Chapter 3

I CHRISTEN THEE...LSM-143

After graduation from Signal School in mid-June 1944, I was sent to Charleston, SC where I was assigned to a flat bottom, amphibious vessel referred to as an LSM (*Landing Ship Medium*). We spent the next few days on liberty and watching the builders place the final touches on the ship. When I first saw it, I thought, *"Why have we been assigned to this tiny thing?"* When I had read about or thought about "Navy", I figured I would be assigned to a battleship, or a destroyer, or even an aircraft carrier. This darn thing wasn't prestigious enough. I figured that all that training I had done, and I'll be stuck on this thing. But, these little amphibious ships turned out to be one of the most important workhorses of the US Navy fleet in World War II. They received no accolades after the war, but the crews and the vessels did their duty like noble sailors. We were all assigned to a crew. Not one of us knew what an LSM was. We didn't know what they looked like, didn't know anything about it. Specifically, I was assigned to the USS LSM-143, affectionately referred to later by the crew as the *"Pickle Barge"* – I'll explain a little more about that later.

Landing Ship Mediums were amphibious assault ships of the United States Navy during World War II. These amphibious vessels carried and deployed men, tanks, trucks loaded with flamethrower fuel, and any other provision or equipment required during beach landings to the shores of islands during the war in the Pacific and the European Theater of Operations (ETO). When I talk about "carry" and "deploy", I mean we slid the ship right up onto the sand, or coral rock, or whatever the surface happened to be. Hopefully the surface was nice smooth sand. However, that wasn't always the case. By design, the hull of LSM had no keel and was angled in such a way as to keep the ship somewhat level when ran upon the beach. This was well and good on paper, but we were at the mercy of every beach that we slid upon. Each beach had its own personality - some were kind and others were not. The surf would do its best to push our stern about. We had to learn to deal with these factors. Just like a mortar man had to adjust angles according to land topography and the wind, we would have to learn to adapt.

The LSM had an empty displacement of five hundred thirty long tons and nine hundred long tons loaded. The exact length of the vessel was two hundred three feet, six inches, and thirty four feet across the beam. The draft unloaded was three and one half feet at the forward and seven feet eight inches at the aft. However, the draft fully loaded was six feet four inches at the forward and eight feet three inches at the aft. The draft of any ship was the distance that the hull extends under the water line. All amphibious vessels were obviously known for their shallow drafts. This draft was usually altered by the load, but it could also be manipulated by the ballast tanks located on the port and starboard side. The crew was able to fill the ballast with water at will, or pump the water back out. The water usually had to be pumped out before the extraction from a beach landing.

Landing Ship Mediums were propelled by either two Fairbanks-Morse or two General Motors Cleveland engines turning 2,800 shp (*ship horse power*), direct drive, with two propellers (Navy men called them "*screws*"). Either of these engines was able to propel the ship at a top speed of 13.3 knots fully loaded. The LSM-143 was specifically equipped with the Fairbanks-Morse engines. Perhaps with a different hull design, these ships could have sped through the water at a much faster rate. But, that was not the intentions in the function of the LSM. The screws (*propellers*) were pitched for power not speed. The engine had to push this hulk onto a beach, and yank it right back off. Power was the key to our success.

An LSM was designed with an "open" well deck. This means that from the conning tower, one could see down into the lower deck at all times. There was no forward upper deck or elevator like those present on the larger LST (*Landing Ship, Tank*). Therefore, the LSM could be loaded quicker and deployed to the beaches much faster than the LST. The open well deck was at capacity when it was loaded with five medium tanks or three heavy tanks (one hundred fifty tons maximum payload, beaching) or six LVTs (*Landing Vehicle Tracked*) or nine DUKWs (six-wheel amphibian idiomatically referred to as a "*Duck*"). It was able to transport and off-load fifty-four combat troops with a complement of four officers and fifty-eight enlisted men manning the ship. The LSM-143 was armed with five single 20mm anti-aircraft (AA) gun mounts and one twin 40mm AA gun mounted on the bow.

There were five hundred fifty-eight LSMs (*Landing Ship, Medium*) made for the United States Navy between 1943 and 1945. The majority of vessels built on this versatile frame were regular transports; however there were several dozen that were converted during construction for specialized roles such as the LSM(R). The LSM(R) (*Land Ship Medium, Rockets*) were utilized for supporting fire during amphibious operations. The vessels were able to maneuver close to shore to deliver fire from rocket launchers mounted on an added upper deck absent on the LSMs. These ships were not normally used to land on the beach, but with the shallow draft, they could navigate closer to shore than other fire supporting ships. Their ability for close proximity to the shore and high trajectory ordinances allowed for targeting the enemy in otherwise protected positions. Most LSMs and LSM(R)s were scrapped during the Cold War, but several were sold by the United States Department of Defense to foreign nations or private shipping companies.

Only one LSM, USS LSM-45 was known to still exist in its original configuration until just early in 2014. It was in storage at Marine Station Camp Lejeune in Jacksonville, NC. The LSM-45 was slated to become the centerpiece of the Museum of the Marine, but due to changed plans, it was scrapped in February of 2014. What an unbearable fate for such a historically significant machine.

***

We clambered aboard this small LSM and down the ladder to the sleeping quarters. Once I walked through the door, there was a narrow passageway barely wide enough for two sailors to walk by each other. I looked around the sleeping quarters at

all the racks stacked four-high along the wall. I chose the very top bunk on the end, and tossed my sea bag. I noticed the smell of oil and diesel that permeated the entire craft. I thought to myself that it was the familiar smell of all ships. I immediately took an ownership to this little ship and its "Navy smell". It's the same feeling you get when you play on a baseball team. You put the uniform on, you take the field, and you do your part to not let the other fellows down. I

wasn't about to let the fellows down. I realized that I was meant to be on this ship, and we would have at least some significance in this big war. At the time, I didn't have a clue of the magnitude of our contribution. But I came to the realization that we would do our part whether we were on an esteemed aircraft carrier or a modest landing ship.

The LSM-143 was commissioned at 1330 hours on 30 June 1944, moored alongside the USS LSM-142, in Pier A, Noisette Creek, Charleston, South Carolina. I was listed as Garforth, Delmar D, S3c(SM) (Seaman Third Class, Signalman) among the alphabetical roster of the crew that reported for our first muster call on the tank deck that day donned in our Navy white dress uniform. The uniform was solid white with a navy blue

neck tie. My left sleeve bore the Signalman Third Class service patch. The patch was embodied with the eagle insignia, cross signal flags, and the Third Class stripe. Fifty-seven other enlisted men and eight officers on board joined me at attention that day while Captain G.E. Baker, USN, officially commissioned the ship into US Naval service. Lieutenant Robert C White read his orders aloud to the crew and assumed duty as commanding officer of the LSM-143. Then, the names of each crew member were read aloud along with each man's rating. The base chaplain read some scripture and said a prayer for the safety of the men on board, then presented Lieutenant White with a bible inscribed with "US Navy" in gold letters on the cover. Lieutenant White turned to the men at the flag mast and ordered the colors and the commission pennant raised, and directed Ensign Lawrence O Nassett, Executive Officer, to set the watch.

The "Champagne Lady" stated the christening vow, "*In the name of the United States, I christen thee LSM-143*". Without delay, she swung back and smacked the bow with the bottle; smashing it instantaneously. The glass flew like shrapnel as an

explosion of the effervescent liquid streamed in every direction. Lieutenant White then dismissed the men at 1400 hours as the commissioning party left the ship to begin the commissioning ceremony on the LSM-142.

With the superstitious portion of the inauguration complete, and before we could get our uniforms dirty, we were called to muster and lined up along the well deck for our crew photograph. Our placement in the photo is described as follows:

The officers were seated in the middle of the front row as the rest of us took our places by rank. I just kneeled down as the last guy on the right in the photo on the front row right next to "Doc" Mallchok. "Doc", our corpsman, was the last guy to get a seat on that big bench that they placed next to the wall of the well deck. He barely fit, and had to hang onto the back of the bench with his right arm just to stay in place. The other signalman, George Cimbala, is the first guy on the left in the fourth row. Verlin "Georgia" Smith, our ship's "*jester*" and pointer for the twin 40mm gun mount, is the first guy on the left in the second row. Don't be fooled by Verlin's seemingly calm demeanor in this photo, this Georgia boy was a REAL nut! The tall guy dead center in the very back is Eldon Hibbard. Eldon was our radioman from Illinois, and a really nice fellow. Bill Schorer and Jim Romano were standing directly in front of Eldon as he peered over their shoulders. Bill and Jim were members of our 20mm gun crews. They were great shots and really good guys. We were all pretty much at ease in the photo. We weren't ordered to stand at attention like we did at muster roll. It appears much like a high school photograph of a class of boys. That's kind of what we were. We were all about the same age, and we were about to embark on the greatest education we could ever receive from any institution. You can look at us and tell that we had no idea just how much this "education" would change our lives.

The officers seated left to right on the front row of the photo were: Ensign James Juliana from New Jersey - communications officer, Ensign John Merschel from Michigan - engineering officer, Captain Robert White from New York – our commanding officer, Ensign Lawrence Nassit from North Dakota - executive officer (XO), and Ensign Stanley Bryan from California assumed the duties of the gunnery officer.

These officers were well respected by the crew while treating the men with respect, dignity and honor. Orders were given devoid of sarcasm and with a gracious quality without fail. Ensign John Merschel was a fellow Michigan boy and we had many enlightening conversations about life back home. Ensign Juliana would take it upon himself, after the war, to get as many of the crew together for reunions and periodically provide a newsletter with current events and upcoming reunions. I got to know all of them very well as I would be stationed next to one of them each time I took my place on the conning tower. Our entire ship roster was as small as a high school football team, and it was pretty easy to get to know every man on the ship.

53

General Quarters!

The YT-177 tug pulled alongside the LSM-143 and moored port side. The LSM-143 was slowly tugged to a docking area in Pier A where the ship could be tested, inspected, and provisioned. The YT-177 cast off the line and gingerly pulled away to do the same for the LSM-142 once it had been properly commissioned.

At 1450 hours, the crew in the engine room was ordered to turn over the engines for the first time. Mechanics gave the engine a thorough inspection to make sure that all systems ran properly.

Ammunition loading commenced just as the engine inspection was completed. The ammunition depot delivered 8,640 rounds of 20mm AA HET (*Anti-Aircraft, High Explosives with Tracers*), 17,250 rounds of 20mm AA HEI (*Anti-Aircraft, High Explosives, Incendiary*), and 180 rounds of 20mm AA BL&P (*Anti-Aircraft, Blind, Loaded, and Plugged: non-explosive rounds used for training*).

Inspections and repairs continued throughout the remainder of the day and into 1 July. The TY-22 tugged the fuel barge alongside the LSM-143 to deliver the first fuel stores for the ship at 2250 hours that evening. After 37,960 gallons of fuel was received, the YT-22, with the fuel barge in tow, pulled away to fuel the next ship on its register for the day.

Deperming, or *degaussing*, is a procedure for erasing the permanent magnetism from ships and submarines to camouflage them against magnetic detection vessels and enemy marine mines.

A sea-going metal-hulled ship or submarine, by its very nature, develops a magnetic signature as it travels, due to a magneto-mechanical interaction with the Earth's magnetic field. This signature can be exploited by magnetic mines, or facilitate the detection of a submarine by ships or aircraft with magnetic anomaly detection (MAD) equipment. Navies use the deperming procedure, in conjunction with degaussing, as a countermeasure for this phenomenon.

The specialized deperming facility in Charleston was used to perform the procedure. The LSM-143 proceeded and docked at the deperming slip at 1400 hours, 2 July. Heavy gauge copper cables encircled the hull and superstructure of the ship, and very high electrical currents (as high as 4,000 amperes) were pulsed through the cables. This had the effect of "resetting" the ship's magnetic signature. It was also possible to assign a specific signature that was best suited to the particular area of the world in which the ship will operate. But over time, the deperm began to degrade, and the procedure would be redone periodically to maintain the desired effect. Two and one half hours after entering the deperming dock, the procedure was complete and the LSM-143 was underway once again.

The following day, more testing took place with the crew of the 143, including opening and closing the bow doors and lowering the ramp for the first time. This was performed at the same time the stern anchor was tested. Each item worked to perfection and testing was complete. The ramp was raised and the bow doors closed. The stern anchor was ordered raised by the captain in preparation for the first test firing of the 20mm guns.

At 0948 hours, the ship was underway and passed through the submarine net and into the open Atlantic Ocean. A course was set to get a safe distance from shore even though the rounds used in this test were to be the 20mm BL&P "blanks" that were loaded the day before. At 1253 hours, Ensign Bryan at his post on the conning tower pressed the General Quarters button. Immediately, the steady, rhythmic horn blasts begins, as he announces over the intercom:

"General Quarters! General Quarters! All hands to battle stations! All hands to battle stations!"

Each of the five gun crews raced to their stations and methodically loaded one magazine of the 20mm BL&P rounds into their respective 20mm AA guns. A navy plane towing a target sleeve appeared and the captain ordered all starboard guns to open fire. Wearing the regulation flak helmets, the four man crews safely swung the guns around toward the open Atlantic, and opened fire. The first time we witnessed all of the guns firing at the same time sent goose bumps all over. It really got our adrenaline pumping. Even though we knew that the rounds were just blanks, it still provided a great show. From the conn, it gave me a rush of pride that this little ship could take care of business if the need arose. At the time, we didn't know if we would be firing at the German Bf-109 or the Japanese A6M Zero. From that very moment, I felt confident that we could send either one burning into the sea.

After a successful test of all five guns, Ensign Bryan secured the ship of general quarters over the intercom:

"Secure from general quarters! Secure from general quarters!"

"All hands are to stand down from general quarters!"

"Return to normal duties."

That same afternoon during beaching maneuvers, the anchor winch failed to operate. Ensign Bryan called to the engine crew for *"All ahead slow!"* About a quarter mile from the beach, the command was given to let go the stern anchor. Nothing happened. After several attempts, Ensign Bryan called to stay the course and try to make the landing without the anchor. He had decided that this would be a great test of how well a landing could be done by using just the engines to retract from the beach. Once the ship hit the beach, we could hear the bottom scrape across the sand and the ship skid to a stop. The landing was perfect. We went through the motions of opening the bow doors and lowering the ramp all the way. Then, about five minutes later, the command was given to raise the ramp and close the bow doors. Before we could attempt to back off without the anchor, the crew commenced to pump out

General Quarters!

the ballast tanks. Emptying the ballast tanks allowed the draft on the ship to be less allowing an easier slide off the shore. Then, without a moment to spare, the engine crew was ordered *"All engines full astern!"* The engines revved with all the power they could muster as the gritty sound of sand scrapping along the bottom slowly faded. The ship lurched backward a couple of times as it broke free from the beach. The bow was now free to bob in converse fashion with the stern as the ship backed into the open Atlantic. Without the aid of the stern anchor, a beach retraction is exceedingly difficult, not to mention problematical on the engines.

All other beach landing practice was cancelled and the LSM-143 moored in Pier 352 at the Navy Yard in Charleston, North Carolina. Navy yard mechanics came aboard to begin

the repairs to the winch that operates the stern anchor. By 6 July, the repairs were completed on the winch and the LSM-143 was once again underway in the company and astern of the LSM-142. With its crew of green and inexperienced officers and crew, the LSM-143 left Charleston for amphibious training in Little Creek, VA.

At 1905 hours, I stood at my post on the conning tower. In nostalgia, I gazed starboard at the evening sun reflecting off the Atlantic Ocean. My mind wandered back to those evenings I spent on the Great Lakes with my friends diving for coins. I thought about the countless moments I spent sitting on the beach and gazing out at the way the water reflected the same sun back into my wandering eyes. Would I see those beaches again? I woke to reality, as I contemplated the boys on the ship ahead of us. I scanned the deck of the 143 in the same manner. Were they pondering the same sort of memories?

At 2011 hours that night, the ships passed Fort Sumter, the garrison made famous when the Confederacy fired the first volley of artillery to militarily initiate the War Between the States in 1861. Even though it was dusk, we could see the fort walls and the rocks stacked at the base. The thing that stands out most in my mind is the image of the American flag rising above the fort walls. What an inspiring image to take with us as we moved on to Little Creek, Virginia for our amphibious landing maneuvers.

The flag was more than just a rectangular piece of cloth with forty-eight stars and thirteen stripes that the military made us salute every morning at reveille. It embodied the whole of our beliefs and convictions as Americans. The flag had our upmost respect. If the ship had a rank patch of its own, it would be the American flag. We were a *"United"* States

59

during the war. No one wanted to burn or walk on the flag. We revered it! We loved and respected the values for which it stood. It represented all the folks back home. Every fiber and every stitch was a boy or girl who gave their life for what the flag embodied. Desecrating the flag was like disrespecting those who gave all.

Chapter 4

BECOMING SANDSCRAPERS

On the way to Little Creek, we had exercised at General Quarters on fire and abandon ship drills. We also attended first aid training conducted by the ships corpsman, Michael D. "Doc" Mallchok. We were underway at standard speed for two days until we arrived at Chesapeake Bay at 0841 hours on 8 July 1944. We were still moving astern to LSM-142 as we entered Little Creek Harbor at 1500 hours. As we made our approach into the bay, the tug Atlas came alongside to starboard bow and pulled us into Pier 3.

***

On 16 July 1942, a U.S. Navy truck drove off Shore Drive, the scenic highway along the south shore of the Chesapeake Bay between the resort areas of Ocean View in the City of Norfolk and the small town of Virginia Beach in Princess Anne County. The resort town was located on the shore of the Atlantic Ocean several miles south of Cape Henry, at the entrance to the bay.

Near an inlet called "Little Creek" the truck stopped in a waterlogged bean field of the Whitehurst family's farm. For days thereafter, trucks loaded with lumber and equipment rolled into the area in almost continuous succession. The reason for this mass assault in a bean field twelve miles northeast of Norfolk was that, early in World War II, Navy planners saw a necessity for landing large numbers of American troops on foreign shores in the face of enemy gunfire. That such operations would be difficult was also evident. New methods and techniques in landing troops would have to be developed. Training would be needed before sufficient men were proficient in the complicated art of the amphibious assault, which would enable U.S. troops to drive to the heart of the enemy.

The base was initially established in the farmland of Princess Anne County. During the early phases of World War II, the base was literally a combination of farmland and swamps. Four bases were constructed on this area: Camp Bradford, Camp Shelton, U.S. Naval Frontier Base, and Amphibious Training Base. Camps Bradford and Shelton were named for the former owners of the land.

At first, Camp Bradford was a training base for Navy Seabees, but in 1943 it was changed into a training center for the crews of LSTs (*Landing Ship, Tank*). Camp Shelton was an armed guard training center for bluejackets serving on board merchant ships as gun crews. At the end of World War II it served as a separation center. The Frontier Base was the forwarding center for Amphibious Force personnel and equipment destined for the European Theater. The Amphibious Training Base (*also known as "Little Creek"*) was the center for all types of amphibious training and the training of ship's crews for LSM (*Landing Ship, Medium*), LCI (Landing Craft, Infantry), LCU (*Landing Craft, Utility*), LCM (*Landing Craft, Mechanized*), and LCVP (*Landing Craft Vehicle, Personnel*) boat crews were also trained at Little Creek.

At the new bases, the techniques of training had to be developed from scratch. Facilities for the upkeep of equipment as well as living facilities for personnel were primitive. The newcomers found few buildings and practically no roads or utilities; just bean vines. After various improvisations, along came temporary buildings that were to later give the site some resemblance to a naval base.

In a few months the trained men who were to land fighting forces from Africa to Normandy were ready for sea. During World War II over 200,000 Navy personnel and 160,000 Army and Marine Corps personnel trained at Little Creek.

***

On 9 July 1944, the LSM-142 cast off from the Pier 3 and got underway and we followed it out 35 minutes later. We spent that day exercising General Drills which included the normal fire drills, man overboard drills, and the first aid type classes given by "Doc" Mallchok. However, what made this different was I finally got to run some flag hoisting drills of my own. Our ship had coordinated with the LSM-142 to allow their Signalman and me to practice. Ensign Bryan was in charge that day and called for the ship to be under Condition I Mike. Included in my flag box was a flag representing each letter of the alphabet and each number from zero to nine along with 10 pennants that represented zero to nine. The "M" flag, or "Mike" as it was phonetically referred, was code for *"general quarters"*. In wartime, Condition I or general quarters was the highest alert that the ship or convoy was in *"imminent danger of an enemy attack"*. The flag was square with a white X on a blue field. This would signal that we were under Condition I. Before I hoisted "Mike", I hooked the "S" or "Sugar" flag to the line. This flag was square also with a small solid blue square inside a larger white square. This flag indicated that we were *"conducting a flag hoist drill"*. I would hoist each flag as the rest of the crew ran their drill. Ensign Bryan initiated the fire drill and the fire crew on board came to action while I hoisted the J ("Jig") flag that represents *"I am on fire and have dangerous cargo; keep clear"*. Well, we all had dangerous cargo on our ships. I mean, we were carrying 20mm and 40mm ammunition. I could also see across the water that the LSM-142 had hoisted a square flag with a yellow and a red triangle meeting at the diagonal. This whole drill was a test of my memory, but thankfully, I was able to remember that the "O" ("Oboe") flag meant that the LSM-142 was conducting a *"man overboard"* drill.

At noon on 11 July, we took on an inspector/trainer, Lieutenant J B Mackey who was aboard for a couple of days to perform what the Navy calls a *"shakedown cruise"*. Throughout those two days, he put us through every exercise he could think of while I practiced signaling and flag hoisting. This also included beaching, anchoring, pumping the ballasts, etc. Anything that needed to be tested, he tested it, made one of us test it, and made sure we knew how to operate and test the function. He was very thorough to say the least. He came aboard several more times while we were in Little Creek to run us through zigzaging, turning, circling, and compass calibration.

AKA (*Attack Cargo Ships*) were U.S. Navy ships designed specifically to carry troops, heavy equipment and supplies in support of amphibious assaults, and to provide naval gunfire support during those assaults. As amphibious operations became more important in World War II, planners saw the need for a special kind of cargo ship, one that could carry both cargo and the LCM and LCVP boats with which to attack the beach, and that carried guns to assist in anti-air defense and shore bombardment. Specifications were drawn up, and beginning in early 1943, the first sixteen U.S. attack cargo ships were converted from Navy cargo ships that had previously been designated AK. A total of one hundred eight of these ships were built between 1943 and 1945—which worked out to an average of one ship every eight days. This speaks volumes about the dedication of the folks back home who worked day and night to provide us with the war machines we needed to defeat the Japanese. "Rosie the Riveter" was a REAL American hero. Many of the AKAs were converted from non-military ships, or started out as non-military hulls. Six additional AKAs, featuring new and improved designs, were built in later years. During World War II the ships were referred to as Attack Cargo Ships and designated *AKA*. In 1969, they were renamed as Amphibious Cargo Ships and re-designated *LKA*.

Compared to other cargo ship types, these ships could carry landing craft, were faster, had more armament, and had larger hatches and booms. Their holds were optimized for combat loading, a method of cargo storage where the items first needed ashore were at the top of the hold, and those needed later were lower down. Because these ships went into forward combat areas, they had Combat Information Centers and significant amounts of equipment for radio communication, neither of which were present in other cargo ships.

Attack cargo ships played a vital role in the Pacific War, where many were attacked by kamikazes and other aircraft, and several were torpedoed. None were sunk or otherwise destroyed.

Becoming Sandscrapers

The main task of the day for 14 July was to work with three other LSMs to beach tanks, halftracks, flamethrower fuel trucks, and other equipment needed for beach assault landings. The 143 was the third ship in the column astern the LSM-261 and the LSM-142, and followed closely by the LSM-211. As they all prepared to go alongside their respective cargo ships, the LSM-143 had orders to moor alongside an AKA and take aboard four Army Sherman tanks and one Army halftrack. I hoisted the yellow square flag with a black circle in the center. This flag announced condition "I" (Item) which signaled to the AKA that we were approaching and our ship was *coming alongside*. The AKA had prepared the first tank and already had it in boom. When the LSM was moored along the port side, the thirty-three ton M4 Sherman was lifted with the massive cables and lowered all the way down into the 143's open deck. The men aboard the AKA then maneuvered each piece of hardware into position, hooked it up, and boosted the massive weapons out and into the well deck. The last to go into the well deck near the door was the nine-ton M3A1 halftrack.

Upon detachment from the AKA, we made our way into the beach at various speeds. The tide was running near high. The water was white-capping as it pounded the shore, and the undertow was racing down the beach. As we approached, the stern anchor was launched about three hundred feet out, and we headed to the beach. The ships had a difficult time not being wave driven sideways onto the beach. The stern anchors were not holding onto the loose sandy bottom. The breakers were undermining the bow holds on the beach. We knew if we got sideways, we would have to be towed off the beach for sure. Well, when the ship made the run, the stern began to slide around to starboard. Immediately, the orders were to winch the anchor and back off. We wheeled the ship around before the stern could come around and get stuck, and we motored back out to sea to give it another try. Evidently the anchor didn't dig in well enough, and we had too much slack to hold the ship straight. We circled around and headed back toward the beach again. We let go the anchor just a few feet later than before and headed into the beach once again. The bottom slid across the grinding sand and slowed to a stop. The bow doors swung open, and the hefty ramp crashed to the sand. The first to disembark was the halftrack. Then, all four engines on the Shermans roared to life. In a single file procession, they tracked down the ramp, and onto the sandy shore. The second time's a charm, as they say. Then, amongst the triumph a reality hit me. In a few weeks or months, we would be doing this for real. Men would die. I might die. Finally, I was shaken to reality by the command to raise the ramp and close the bow doors, and I realized that it was not a good idea to dwell on my mortality. It was way too easy to acquire a fatalistic view of your future. The anchor's winch clicked into gear and the engines whined full astern as the sandy grind scratched along the bottom of the ship like a cat on a metal screen door. The ship slowly turned, weighed the stern anchor, and steamed to the open sea.

The rest of our time in Little Creek, was spent in countless mock landings of equipment and troops. These landings were completed in collaboration with the group we had started with on the fourteenth. We had several times at Little Creek where we had to abort a landing and just try again. Landing an LSM on a beach was not as easy as pulling up on the sand and putting the engines in reverse to get back off. The proper procedure went something like this:

With our well deck full of Marines and/or equipment, we would motor full steam toward the beach. Within five hundred feet of the beach, we would open the bow doors. Our ship would let go the stern anchor, and pay out the cable about two hundred feet. Not only was the anchor used to pull the ship back off the beach, but it ensured that the stern did not swing the ship sideways. If it got sideways to the beach, it was liable to be there for an eternity. We dragged that anchor some to get it to dig in as we landed. I mean, we would drive right onto the beach. We had to keep the engines ahead slow while we were beached to pull against the anchor and keep the ship from broaching. To add even more stability, the ballast tanks near the bow were filled. Then, the ramp would be lowered to allow the Marines, tanks, or trucks to maneuver ashore. When we pulled up onto the beach, it formed a powerful suction to where the engines could not pull the ship back off the beach by themselves. When the last of the cargo exited the well deck, the front ballast tanks were emptied. The winch would be engaged to pull against the anchor and the engines set at full reverse. The ship would pretty much heave around on the stern anchor.

Unfortunately, there were times when the anchor and the engines were not enough to get a ship off the beach. Another ship might have to be used, perhaps another LSM, to help pull. Therefore, an exercise that proved to be quite meaningful in combat was the art of towing another ship. When a ship is beached on purpose, even one that was designed for the job, things invariably go wrong at one time or another. Engine failures and winch damage could leave a landing ship stranded like a beached whale. The LSM-142 was our partner in this endeavor, and we practiced real-world scenarios. These included towing a ship in open waters, and towing one that is stuck on a beach. Our ship would be placed in condition "Z" (Zebra) and the flag with four triangles in the colors red, black, blue and yellow arranged in a square was hoisted meaning; "*I require a tug.*"

Flag hoisting drills were also conducted with LSM-211 as our days went by in Little Creek. We always took our third spot in the four-ship column as we all went through group training. All four ships had been ordered to perform test firing on all the 20mm guns on board our ships. Each of the first two guns fired beautifully without a hitch. When we got around to what we referred to as Gun #6, the gun jammed. After removing the magazine and clearing the jam, the gunners open fired once again without a problem.

21 July rolled around and we were ordered to test the engines to their fullest capacity. The nautical term for this was flank speed. Flank speed referred to the engines true maximum speed. This was generally reserved for situations that were considered imminent danger, such as bombing raids or strafing. However, due to the known limits of the engines, these speeds were not sustainable for long periods of time. It was known to cause excessive fuel consumption and possibly engine failure. The LSM-143 proceeded from the bay and was ordered to full speed until it came to a good cruising speed. Then, flank speed was ordered and the 143 sustained this for fifteen minutes until it was ordered back down to two thirds speed. The twin Fairbanks-Morse engines held up well with no engine problems.

***

Twenty-three other men and I went on leave on 25 July to take in the scenery of the town of Norfolk, Virginia. These men had been there since the eighth and had not stepped foot from the ship. A leave was a welcomed respite. The boys toured the town and were due back seventy-two hours later. I made sure that I was back in seventy-one hours just so I didn't have to hear it from Lieutenant White. However, thirteen of the twenty-three who left on the twenty-fifth weren't so diligent. Lieutenant White held mast at 0900 on the thirty-first of July in the presence of his aboard ship court. He gave each man his sentence for the crime of absence over leave (*AOL*). Most of the men were gigged with the loss of five to ten liberties depending on the amount of time the sailor was late. A majority was also tacked on extra hours of KP (*kitchen patrol*) duty, latrine duty, or any other unpleasant jobs he could conjure.

I made sure I was back an hour early not only because of the Captain, but what I remember reading in *"Offenses Against Military Law"* section of the *"The Bluejackets' Manual"*. It covered the severity of the offense of AOL and alluded to the degree of a sailor's loyalty. It stated: *"a man who intentionally refrains from returning on time in order to pursue some diversion which he fancies to be more important than his positon in the service testifies to his slight regard for his military obligation"*. In my opinion, being derelict of one's duty reflected badly on personal character and could have been a disgrace to family as well. I didn't want that hanging over my head. There was more to think about than one's self in the military. Our lives depended largely on our character and commitment to each other. A sailor had to think about the guys around him. Trust was imminent in the heat of battle. There was no time for absentees. Not only was the possible punishment the withholding of the next liberty, but they could also dock part or all of the next paycheck. I couldn't afford to do without even part of what meager pay that we had received from the Navy. Being AOL wasn't an option for me; I wanted the officers and the other men to know I could be trusted. I enjoyed the time I was on liberty, but I was going to be at my post. I was going to do my duty.

On 2 August we had moored into the Deperming Station at Lambert's Point Virginia for our second time since the 143 had been commissioned. While we were here, Lieutenant White felt that it was a good time to hold another mast for three AOL cases that happened the day before. One of the boys, James Romano, S2c, was AOL for an hour and ten minutes and would not stay out of trouble until we got into combat. Arthur Haverly had been out with Romano and was AOL for his first and only time for an hour and ten minutes. Wilbert Washington, "Willie" as we all knew him, was AOL for four hours and fifteen minutes. Willie was an African-American boy that kept us in stitches all of the time. He was really a wise-cracking, funny guy, and a lot of fun to be around. Unfortunately, he had gotten into too much fun this time and lost some liberty like the other two. Two hours later, we pulled from the deperming station and moored at Pier C, Craney Island, to take on 17,275 gallons of diesel oil.

At 2235 hours, 6 August, we were awakened by the sound of men yelling for the corpsman. When I got to the top, one of our boys, Harvey Hobert, RM3c, was bleeding badly from his forehead and nose. Doc Mallchok got to Harvey quickly and began to place bandages on his wounds to stop the bleeding. A couple of men from the LSM-139 had told the officer of the deck (*OOD*), Ensign Jim Juliana, that they had carried him up a few yards away from the main gate where Harvey had been fighting with another sailor. They told Ensign Juliana that the other sailor in the fight was still at the main gate being held by the guard.

Juliana calmly walked down to the main gate and questioned the guard about the incident. The guard was alone at the time and stated that it was too dark to tell what had happened, but he had heard an argument, then a loud scuffle between a couple of men. Then, John Lurding, Coxswain, emerged from the darkness stumbling toward the main gate. The guard reported that he was drunk, his clothes filthy, and devoid of proper identification. The guard then stated that Lurding staggered away again ignoring orders to halt.

By this time Ensign Juliana was not as calm. He strode down to the dock to find John sitting with his back and head resting on a post. This guy had been on a real bender all night long. John was three sheets to the wind with no hope for the sails to be secured. He had downed so much hooch, he couldn't even stand.

"Off and on sailor!"

This was a command from NCOs and officers that we had heard dozens of times in boot camp. It simply meant for you to get "off" your behind and "on" your feet immediately. And that's the clean translation.

"Get back to the ship Lurding! You are absent over leave sailor!"

"No can do, sir!"

"If you don't get off my deck and back to your rack right now, I'll have you put in the brig!"

"Suit yourself, sir."

Juliana wheeled around to the guard and requested that he call the Shore Patrol. Ten minutes later, Lurding was in custody and taken to the brig.

Back on the ship, Doc Mallchok diagnosed Hobert's condition as a possible skull fracture. When Juliana got back to the ship and got word from Doc Mallchok that Hobert needed further treatment, he called the base ambulance to get him to the hospital.

Three of the boys who had been found guilty of AOL in the 29 July mast, Ed Bush (S2c), John Lurding (Cox), and Harvey Hobert (RdM3c) were out together again painting the town. That time, Ed Bush returned on time, but Lurding and Hobert were absent over leave once again. Ed had left to return to the ship way before the altercation broke out between Lurding and Hobert, so he had no details about what caused the brawl.

Harvey Hobert was injured so badly that he would not return to the LSM-143 until just before we pulled out for Key West, Florida. John Lurding was brought back on board the very next morning at around 1030 hours and was tried by captain's mast. Lurding testified that it was just a misunderstanding over a *"dame"* after both boys had a few too many beers. Lieutenant White elected to give Lurding sixteen hours extra duty with a loss of ten liberties. Lurding and Hobert would have to get passed their differences if they were to spend time together on a ship this small. When the bullets start flying, there is no time for internal conflict.

It was later found that James Romano, who had been found guilty of being AOL just a week before, was also found guilty of placing an improper entry into the log. He was fined thirty-six dollars pay over three months. The ironic aspect of this was that Romano placed an entry that he was given permission for leave on the day he was absent over leave. We were all kids who were expected to grow up really fast. We had too. We had a job to do. I'm not making up excuses for their actions at Little Creek. But, John and James were men you could count on when duty called. They were good sailors.

With all the drama of boys behaving badly behind us, we added a new weapon to our arsenal. While docked in the yard of Little Creek a twin 40mm gun mount and ammo magazine was installed on the bow of the ship. We had wondered when we first came aboard as to why we only had the 20mm guns. We had trained in boot camp on the 20mm and the 40mm anti-aircraft guns. It made the ship look like a real war machine with those twin babies on the bow. She had some real muscle now, and we knew the LSM-143 could really put a hole in something that came asking for it.

Chapter 5

BOUND FOR THE PACIFIC

At 1029 hours, 13 August, 1944, the LSM-143 weighed anchor from Hampton Roads, Virginia underway to ports in Key West, Florida. The sparkling water reflected the midmorning sun casting its rays from the eastern sky. The rumbling of the engines gave a comforting living, breathing characteristic to the ship. The screws mixed the water into a white froth like a swimmer kicking his legs in a race. The LSM-143 was alive, and I had never felt more alive. I was seventeen and a sailor, and I loved everything about the water. I had lived around it all of my life. It was a part of me. It was in my soul. Now, the Navy was in my spirit. It was woven into me. As I gazed down into the clear Atlantic, I wondered if I could dive to the bottom like my friends and I had done all of those times in Lake Michigan. I pondered if I could catch any fish out of that water that tasted as good as those blue gills I used to snag. The crunch of the fried perch that my Mom would cook made my mouth water just from the vision in my mind's eye.

A couple of hours underway, I looked to our starboard side, and in the distance, I saw the Cape Henry Lighthouse. What a beautiful structure: the lighthouse. It stood tall like a guardian. A lighthouse never wavers. Its beacon was a protector of sailors; keeping us from running aground. It guided us along. The lighthouse reassured us that it will be there when we came back. It called me home to Ludington North Pierhead in Michigan where I spent my days swimming and fishing near the breakwater.

On the sixteenth, we passed two lightships as we traveled down the Georgia and Northern Florida coast. The Savannah Lightship was moored just to our starboard side when we passed it in the morning at 1024 hours. Later that evening at 1905 hours,

we passed the St John's Lightship (LV-84) to our starboard. This time, the lights on both masts were shining bright in the evening sky. Lightships were vital partners with America's lighthouses as part of the federal government's commitment to safe navigation on the nation's coasts and on the Great Lakes. While the first American lighthouse dates to the colonial era, the use of lightships is a more recent 19th century spectacle in the United States. Lightships were manned by a full crew and equipped with radar to warn when approaching ships were venturing too close to perilous zones along the coast. They were generally moored over treacherous reefs, or marking the narrow approaches to a channel or harbor entrance where lighthouses could not be built. When the radar man saw the necessity, he would sound the crew to stations and the ship would provide caution to the approaching vessel. As opposed to the estimated one thousand five hundred lighthouses utilized along our coastal waters and the Great lakes, there were only

one hundred seventy-nine lightships built between 1820 and the 1952.

On the seventeenth and eighteenth, we passed thirteen or more lighthouses and reef towers along the way that kept us clear of land and out of danger. However, there are tons of reefs along the coast of the Florida Keys. Just a few miles north of Key Largo is an area called Triumph Reef. The Fowey Rocks Light

Tower was built on the reef like several other towers in this part of the Floridian coastal waters. We had passed this tower to our starboard and altered our course to attempt to avoid the reef. We had the engines at standard, around eleven knots, and steaming a little faster than we should have been in that area. We didn't actually run aground, but we literally jumped over something at 2315 hours, on 17 August, and hit it pretty hard. It had to be a reef, but no one knew for sure. Lieutenant Merschel, OOD at the time, went below and assessed that we only sustained relatively minor damage and that we should be able to make it to our port in the Keys. With a heightened tone of caution, we were underway.

In the dark early morning hours of the eighteenth, we kept our engines ahead one-third to avoid running across another reef with the 143. Once we experienced day break, and we could visually see the reefs, the engines were ordered at standard speed. Throughout the morning, we had passed several more reef light towers and were just entranced by the magnificence of these shallow waters while at the same time humbled by the dangers of running aground on a reef again. I had become more suspicious when I saw large shadows or color variations in the water. I felt that I had to make sure that we didn't run upon another reef. With the light towers appearing more and more often, I knew the reefs were a valid concern.

At 1350 hours, Friday, 18 August, the LSM-143 eased into

Craig Docks, Berth 6, at Key West, Florida, and moored starboard side of the USS LSM-145. Later that afternoon, we took on provisions including stores of food necessary for general mess that were inspected and approved for quality and quantity by Doc Mallchok. The food supplies included milk, Bisquick flour, jam, egg noodles, peanut butter, various cans of soup, and various fresh fruits and vegetables.

On the morning of 19 August, 1944, the LSM-141 arrived at Craig Dock and moored alongside to port. The LSM-143 spent one week at Key West, Florida getting the necessary inspections and repairs to assure seaworthiness after that run-in we had with the reef.

Thursday, 24 August, saw the LSM-143 launched as the third ship in a column of four LSMs toward our next destination, the Panama Canal. The LSM-143 made way in column astern of the LSM-212 and the LSM-142, and followed in column by the LSM-314. By midmorning, we had passed to starboard the Sand Key Light and the Marquesas Rock Light towers. At noon, bearing eight miles south of the Marquesas Rock Light tower, the engines were orders all ahead flank at seven hundred eighty RPM. We steamed at this rate for an hour and a half until the engine room was ordered to back down to standard speed at eleven knots. By 1600 hours that afternoon with gorgeous blues skies and aqua marine water, the engines were ordered all ahead full for the rest of the evening.

The next morning saw the crew experimenting with the ballast tanks to find out what combination would make for better travel in certain conditions. The engines were ordered at standard and we ran with all the tanks empty for about an hour. Then, they would fill the center and leave the port and starboard tanks empty and run for an hour. We tried the outside tanks full and the center empty for a period. This testing went on for the next four days until we arrived at the entrance of the Panama Canal.

By 27 August, we had dropped to the tail of the column of the same LSMs with the engines still steaming at standard. By 1500 hours, 28 August, the column was standing into Coco Solo Harbor on various courses and speeds to conform to the

channel. The funny thing is that I remember seeing a lot of buildings around the Atlantic side as we arrived but didn't see any when we exited on the Pacific side. At 1730 hours, the

LSM-143 was instructed to moor on Pier 1B portside to LSM-314 and remained there for the next two days. At this point, we had received more provisions of water and food, including beef tenderloin, chicken, spare ribs, beef stew meat, and various fruits and vegetables. The clock was also set back to +5 time.

During the war, Coco Solo's Naval Aviation Facility served as the base for a P-38 Lightning squadron. FDR had declared the area on 17 December 1941 as the Navy Hospital Area in his Executive Order 8981. Coco Solo would remain under the jurisdiction of the Secretary of the Navy until war's end. The harbor would serve as a refueling and resupplying depot for naval ships on their way to the Pacific.

We spent the night in the canal town of Coco Solo. But a

Aerial view of the US Naval Station, Coco Solo, CZ (Circa 1941)

bunch of us were going to go downtown. We didn't get any farther than the first street until we saw prostitutes. Hundreds of them I suppose. There were buildings with plate glass windows, and they would be right in the window advertising their wares. They would be out on the street, and they would walk up and grab you. Several of us went to a beer garden. It was just a nice setting; beautiful palm trees and a nice view of the canal. No one was checking IDs. A man in a military uniform didn't need an ID. I was drinking beer, but I wasn't old enough. I wasn't even eighteen yet. I didn't turn eighteen until we had left the canal and entered the Pacific. I never drank much, never got drunk. There were a few of us that didn't want any part of it. But, out of fifty-eight men, there were about thirty of them that contracted gonorrhea. I was thankful that I didn't take any part in it. To the sailor who had been infected, it was just one more shot they had to endure. But, this stuff took a few days to cure completely. From that point on, the boys were much more careful when they were on leave. I wasn't there to get drunk. But, hey, if you're a service man and you don't drink, there is something wrong with you - Lots of peer pressure.

At 0927 hours, 30 August, the LSM-143 was underway for the Gatun Locks as the third ship in a column of four once again. Except, this time, she was astern of the LSM-142 and LSM-141, and was followed by the LSM-145. At 1020 hours, the ship was moored port side to the Gatun Locks with two six inch manila lines and was towed through each lock by the electric lock engines. It was quite a thrill watching the way they moved us through the locks. I think there were three locks. We drove into one; they closed a water tight door behind us. Then, they flooded it so that the ship rose to the next level. Then, we went forward into the next level. It's the opposite procedure coming from the Pacific side. It took less than a full day of travel to actually get through the canal. Going through, we had a new appreciation for the difficult job it was to cut through the mountains and jungle to form the canal. I really had the utmost respect for the people who built it.

It took about ten minutes by the time we entered each lock, the gates closed, the lock filled with water, and then we were towed to the next lock. As the lock would fill, the water swirled from the bottom slowly raising the ship to the level of the next lock. By 1119 hours we were disconnected from the towing lines, and were underway and entering Gatun Reach. The LSMs navigated their way around the picturesque islands of Tiger and Las Brujas, then finally through the Penna Blanca Reach. The view was genuinely astounding. The Gatun Bay was filled with so many stunning islands that were spread out as far as the eye could see. Our ship edged around the Barro Colorado Island which was a government reservation for native plants and animals of the area. The Tabernilla Reach emerged into the Frijoles Bay which was dotted with marshes, islands and mangroves and a breeding ground for mosquitos that the crew had to keep at bay.

Countless tropical reaches were passed on the way to the Pedro Miguel and the Miraflores locks. These paradises were a bird watcher's dream with all the exotic birds that skimmed over the water and soared through the jungles. The plant life and animals in the marshes and reaches were simply breathtaking.

We approached the Pedro Miguel locks at 1345 hours, 30 August and exited the final lock at Miroflores at 1540 hours. The canal ship moored alongside the LSM-143 and took off the four canal workmen that guided us through the canal and all the obstacles that we encountered along the way.

By 1600 hours, 30 August, we were standing out of Balboa Canal Zone as the third ship in a column of four, astern the LSM-142 and LSM-141, and followed by the LSM-145 at a distance of five hundred yards between ships. To our port side at a distance of six hundred yards we could see three more LSMs in a column; LSM-211, 212, and 261. It was a thing of beauty to watch us and the six other ships steam toward the Pacific stretching our legs with all ahead full.

The next day, 31 August 1944, I turned eighteen as we steamed about the islands and reefs of Coiba National Park. This collection of thirty-eight islands was well known for its ecological and marine life diversity, and its exquisite white sandy beaches, hardwood tropical forests and wildlife that was exclusive to the area. It was an awe inspiring site for a boy officially aging into manhood. I had gotten a letter from my family a few days earlier wishing me a happy birthday and telling me all about what was happening back home. I read the letters over and over. It was great to read a letter from my dad especially. He didn't have much to say in person, but his letters were heartwarming and sincere. He was always the gentlest man that I had ever known. I thought back at the times he would rub my legs at night trying to relieve the pain from the Chorea I had when I was a kid. He never said a word but he would hum a soothing tune while he rubbed. I think the melody did more for the pain than anything. I replayed the tunes in my head while admiring the beauty of the Pacific seascape. It would be my soundtrack. It would be my connection to home when that longing came over me. This was the first time that I had a birthday without my family. I missed them. But, I knew this was something I had to do. All of us boys at that time had a sense of duty to our country. I knew I would have been miserable at home while history was being made during my generation. I had to be part of it.

As day broke, my eyes turned to port and I was mesmerized by the shear vastness and indescribable beauty of the Pacific Ocean. I'm not sure as an eighteen year old kid that I completely appreciated the majesty of this massive body of water that God had bestowed on us humans and millions of sea creatures. I was awestruck, nevertheless, that I was looking at the Pacific Ocean for the first time. Little did I know, at the time, that I would be skimming across this entire wavy seascape in a two hundred three foot amphibian. *"Is this thing as bullet-proof as I am?"* Most eighteen year old men have this perception of their fate. I had that much confidence in the 143, and I had that much confidence in myself. I knew we would go over there and kick those Nips' butts all the way back to Japan. Fifty-seven other boys felt the same way I did. I could see it when I looked at them. We were the "Navy". Nobody could stop us - Nobody.

Del at his post enroute to the Pacific

Chapter 6

PRACTICE FOR WAR

From 9 September through 2 November, the LSM-143 joined many other ships in San Diego for operations off the coast of the island of San Clemente. Just after completing mess on 1 September, general quarters was sounded, yet again, to exercise drills. Over the intercom system, the following order:

"General quarters! General quarters!"

"All hands provide and equip for abandon ship!"

"All hands provide and equip for abandon ship!"

So, immediately I hoisted the "Sugar" (*flag hoist drill*) and the "Oboe" (*abandon ship*) flags to the yardarm. All hands rushed to their life jackets. During the abandon ship drills, each man had to carry out a particular duty. In the event of sinking, the officer on deck had to gather the deck log and throw it overboard. A log book was weighted heavy enough to sink to the bottom if thrown overboard. We didn't want the enemy to gain possession of the log books and use the information against us. In case of a real emergency, each life raft would be equipped with emergency rations, mess gear, water breakers, medical kit, boat box, Very's pistol and stars, signal flags, rifles and ammunition.

General Quarters!

After we had secured from abandon ship drills, about fifteen minutes later, we began fire drill. I hoisted the "Jig" (*ship's afire*) flag along with the "Sugar" flag to let the other ships know that we were under a fire drill, and that it was only a drill. Orders were given to stop all fresh air blowers and close valves, ports, doors, and hatches once all personnel had been accounted for. Stopping the air flow throughout a ship helped to deprive a fire of oxygen. On deck, it was hard enough to control a fire with the constant ocean breezes blowing across; feeding the fire its life-sustaining oxygen. Care had to be taken not to cut off or close unnecessarily the passages and hatches used for access and for communication.

The men also had to remove anything flammable or explosive in the vicinity of the fire. The ship was equipped with a gasoline powered pump that could be used to pump out flooded compartments or to aid in firefighting situations. This was piped to a manifold that could handle several fire hoses at once if necessary. It used the sea water that was supplied by suction lines hung over the side of the ship. It could bring about 2,400 gallons of water per minute at one hundred pounds of pressure to fight a fire. This was a test of how quickly our fire crew could get to the machine, get it hooked up, cranked up, and deploy the water off the side of the ship. They sprayed it over the side of the ship to test pressure and flow distance. We sprayed it down into the well deck sometimes to make us a "swimming pool", but not during exercises. A fire will die if deprived of one of the three main elements: fuel, oxygen, or heat.

Once we were secured from general quarters, the ballast tanks were checked, and the port and starboard tanks were pumped empty. Then, the center tank was filled with 2,400 gallons of sea water to add stability to the LSM-143 carrying a light cargo. We had taken aboard five thirty-six foot LCVPs from an APA while we were docked in Norfolk, Virginia on 12 August. Five LCVPs didn't weigh anywhere near as much as five Sherman tanks. So, we considered that a "light" load. With the center ballast tank full, Lieutenant Merschel ordered the engines ahead full as we continued our course to San Diego. Many times we would pump water in and out of the ballast tanks depending on the situation. If we had a full well deck, we would generally empty all the tanks especially on approach to a beach landing. Also if the weather was bad, full ballast tanks would lower our center of gravity and keep us from capsizing. We mainly had to tinker with the tank levels to get the right amount of ballast when we were underway on an empty well deck. When the ballast was correct, the LSM-143 would skid across the water almost effortlessly.

A pod of curious common dolphins appeared out of nowhere just below the surface and then all at once, vaulted from the surf. Intrigued by the resonance of the screws sloshing up the foam from the stern, they leapt and dived, over and over. These were beautiful animals with a deep gray body and a broad creamy white stripe down both sides. The dolphin is a majestic animal, and it was amazing to witness it overcome drag to race next to the ship at the speeds it could attain. It reminded me of a dog in the way it seemed to do its best to be social with humans. The captain thought he would make it a better race, so he ordered the engines to flank. It was a great show watching them streak through the water, then leap for air and do it again. They kept this race up for a few minutes, then veered off toward the open Pacific and disappeared. The LSM-143 was then relegated back on all ahead full.

We test fired the 40mm guns again on 6 September without a hitch, and tested the "Very" guns as well. The Very gun was designed in the late nineteenth century by an American Naval officer named Edward Wilson Very. This gun was commonly known by the layman as the flare gun. Flare guns were used whenever a ship needed to send a distress signal. The flares must be shot directly above, making the signal visible for a longer period of time to reveal the position of the ship in need of assistance.

The Very gun was a 10 gauge, center fire, brass head, and standard paper shotgun shell with primer. The cartridges were red, green, and white, and each had a firing charge of about twenty-five grains of musket powder and a star or stars. The colored cartridges were distinguished by the color and surface of the wad in the end. The stars were packed twelve to a cardboard box, with each cartridge in a separate compartment. The boxes were wrapped with paper and shellacked over to keep out moisture. The Coxswain was responsible for knowing the exact location of the Very gun and how to load and fire the pistol properly. However, the Signalman on board was also trained in the proper use of the gun. We only had two Coxswains on our roster so if one of them weren't on duty; it was up to one of us Signalmen to fire the Very.

Our band of LSMs arrived in San Diego at 1525 hours, on 9 September. With my conning tower looking over the shoulder of the LSM-142 and LSM-141 just to our bow, we could see San Diego Harbor to our starboard. We stood out in the harbor for a few minutes until the LSM-141 had time to moor a port the 142. We carefully idled into the South Creek Pier just to the port side of the LSM-141, when all of the sudden, we felt a jolt. I looked to port to see that we had struck the dock with our bow door on the port side. Ensign Bryan dashed down to the dock after we had moored to discover we had sustained some pretty serious damage to the door. It didn't appear to hurt the dock, and Ensign Bryan immediately had the yard workers aboard no more than three hours later to assess the needed repairs on the door.

The initial testing of the door revealed that the ship had suffered a warp near the hinge. They asked us to back the ship out into the harbor and anchor. When we tried to open the doors, the port side wouldn't budge. After they had completed their assessment of the damage, we were informed that the LSM-143 would have to be taken to the Naval Repair Yard. We had joked around that we hoped this wasn't a bad omen for our first berth on the Pacific coast.

Before we were released to the repair yard, a customs officer came aboard the ship and conducted a thorough inspection. I guess he had to make sure we didn't bring anything aboard illegally during our stay in the Panama Canal. He rummaged through all of our stores including the freezer, ammunition storages, and fuel storage. He searched through anything that resembled a hiding place. I heard later that this was just standard procedure.

Before getting repairs, we had to empty the well deck of the five LCVPs we had been hauling since we were on the East coast. We backed out of Pier 11 enroute to Pier 1 to moor alongside an APA. This time, we took better care to pull in than we did at Pier 11. I don't think Ensign Bryan wanted to explain having the starboard bow door repaired this time. We got the 143 tied to the dock, and the APA maneuvered the crane to offload the five personnel landing craft. With our well deck cleared, we were underway to the Navy Repair Base where we docked at Pier three for the necessary repairs to the bow door.

During the repairs, we took on supplies of food and water

with the Doc's inspections and approval. We also took on new transfers as well. Four of the boys who had traveled with us up to this point, John McClain (RM3c), John Grant (QM3c), James Moulton (MoMM3c), and Thomas Parsons (EM3c) were transferred to the LSM-140. We gained three more men, A.C. Williams (S2c), E. W. Nielson (BM1c), and H.C. Williams (StM2c) who brought their transfer orders and sea bags on board.

We ate really well during our training. We took on boneless beef, chicken, butter, dozens of eggs, smoked ham, lots of fruit, and the list goes on and on. Everything was fresh. Being a small ship, we were constantly at the mercy of our location as to whether or not we had fresh food. We weren't like the larger ships that seemed to have endless freezer space and literally tons of food. We would find out when we got in the middle of the Pacific how good we had it along the east and west coast of America.

On 19 September 1944, Captain J.P.B. Barrett, Commander LSM Third Flotilla, came aboard to give Lieutenant White our ship's orders of transfer to the Fifth Flotilla. At the time, the Fifth Flotilla was under the authority of Commander W.H. Carpenter. The orders included that we would be in LSM Group Fifteen lead by Lieutenant Commander A.H. Hall, and LSM Division Twenty-nine under Lieutenant G.E. Stricker. We would remain in the same flotilla throughout the war, but we were moved around to different groups and divisions as other ships became casualties. A ship can be a "replacement" much like an infantryman or Marine. We just did our duty and followed orders.

Ensign Bryan had been in charge on conn most of the morning of the twenty-second and had brought us to muster to find no absentees. It was a breezy, beautiful September day on deck with just the faint wisp of clouds in the sky. I had just taken my station on the conn at the signal light when the mail call came aboard. I had gotten a letter from my mother speaking of the windy, but pleasant fall weather near the Great Lakes and how my Grandpa was still keeping the old car in ship-shape for me when I return. It was a great comfort to reminisce about those rides that my Grandpa and I had on our way to Ludington when he let me switch with him and drive. When I was away from home, I needed those reminders that things remained as they always were. I reminded myself to trust in God that He would lay His protective hand on me, and bring me back to my family and those lakes that had so many fond memories for me. It was then that I realized why they called those majestic bodies of water *"Great"*. *"Great"* was an understatement though. I don't know if there are adjectives in our vocabulary that can fully describe how exultant those lakes were to me.

Ensign Bryan had received a telegram, and I was distracted from my letter when he began to sob. His mother, Amy, in

Seattle, was deathly ill and she was not expected to recover. He hurried down the ladder to find Captain White, who immediately granted him seven days of emergency leave. Within the hour, he was packed and on his way to the bus station to catch a ride due north to his hometown of Seattle, Washington. The influenza bug caused an epidemic between 1943 and 1944, and many lives were lost because of the spread of this virulent condition. His mother died of pneumonia that she had developed as a result of the virus.

As I watched him leave, I gently folded my letter, slipped it into my pocket, gazed out to port and whispered a quick prayer to God. I didn't just pray for me, I prayed for Ensign Bryan and comfort for him and his mother. I prayed that he would be able to give her a kiss and tell her goodbye one last time. I prayed for all the boys on board the 143 and the other ships I saw moored at their berth. I prayed for the safety and health of my mother, father, sister, and grandpa. And then I thanked God for allowing me to defend this wonderful nation in which I had been abundantly blessed. I pulled the letter out from my pocket and read each word once more as a warm Pacific breeze blew across the conn.

Ensign Bryan hadn't been gone two hours until I heard the clash of metal and felt a slight lurch forward of the ship. I wheeled around expecting a Japanese sub attack only to see the LSM-202 veering off at our stern. The scene was reminiscent of general quarters because every man ran to the deck to investigate the shutter. Ensign Juliana, officer on deck, ran to the stern to assess any damage that he could see. The only thing that he noticed was that the anchor stanchion was bent and the wake light on the back had been broken. The OOD of the LSM-202 noticed that we had not sustained any significant damage, so he just waved his apologies, and proceeded to moor at his assigned area. Juliana presented him an irritated glance, and then shook his head in disgust.

By then, we had gotten quite friendly with the Naval Repair Base. When we arrived they just laughed at us and said,

"Boy, you fellas are always in a pickle!

Wheel that barge in here!"

That's where we got the nickname *"Pickle Barge"*. At the time, that name fit, and it stuck. So far, we had either gotten ourselves out of a "pickle" or gotten some help. That time the yardmen gave us a hand.

Repairs were completed overnight on the anchor stanchion, wake light, and a valve in one of the engines to prepare for our first landing on the Pacific sands. Our next practice was on American soil as we were moored at South Creek Repair Base in San Diego, California. We mustered at 0800 hours with no absentees, and Lieutenant Juliana gave orders to make all necessary preparations for getting underway.

I relieved George Cimbala from his post on the conn after muster call, and made sure he had no unfinished business or dispatches. His answer was *"negative"*, so I read over the file of the past watch for information of dispatches and signals that might need my attention. I made a rapid check of the condition of the flag bag. While I was there, I retrieved the "Zero" flag (*underway in formation*) and began to hoist it up the halliard with rapidity and smoothness as to make sure that the lines remained taut. This was what we were drilled with every day in signalman school:

"Accuracy in bending on the correct flag the first time;

Rapidity in getting up the hoist;

Smoothness in hoisting and quickness in catching a turn with the halliard, and then hauling the downhaul taut, so as to make a straight standing hoist;

Standing up all flags clear;

Visibility of the signal as it goes up, which means keeping a fairly taut downhaul while hoisting; and

Smartness in getting the signal down sharply and smoothly, without allowing them to stream off to leeward, over the side, etc."

We were underway by 0815 hours according to Order number 104-44 to the Marine Base Beach to pick up Marines and tanks. The sky was clear with the sun glistening off the water just as it had done so many times on our trip up the coast. A Pelagic gull shot across our bow and skimmed the water in search of a meal. I followed it off to starboard and noticed it was heading right for this huge, white object in the water. It was hard to tell what it was at first until it turned sideways and started flapping its upper and lower fins against the water. One of the guys from this area identified it as a sunfish. I had never seen one in real life, and the thing was absolutely monstrous. It must have been about ten feet across and about as tall. It came to the surface, and the seagull landed in the water beside the colossal fish to feed upon the countless parasites that plague their skin. The sunfish just hovered at the surface to warm in the sun and enjoy the "back scratch" from the gull.

At 0901 hours, we sounded general quarters for all hands to man their stations. The procedure was business as usual by then. We had done this scores of times at Little Creek, and we approached White Beach by letting go anchor at two hundred feet from shore. With the engines at two thirds, we went head-on to the beach. The white-capped rollers slammed into the white sands as we roared to the beach with no ballast forward. The front rose as the bottom scraped gently across the smooth California sand. We opened the bow doors and lowered the ramp that crashed to the beach. The Marines were waiting on shore and drove three M4A1 Shermans, fifteen enlisted men, and one lieutenant trudged across the bow ramp and into our well deck. Within just seven minutes we had loaded, raised the ramp, closed the bow doors, and retracted from the beach. The LSM-143 wheeled around and maneuvered in position as the third ship in a column of four with the LSM-236, LSM-141, and the LSM-145. The engines were ordered at all ahead full with an interval of two hundred yards between ships. Our next destination: Pyramid Cove, San Clemente Island.

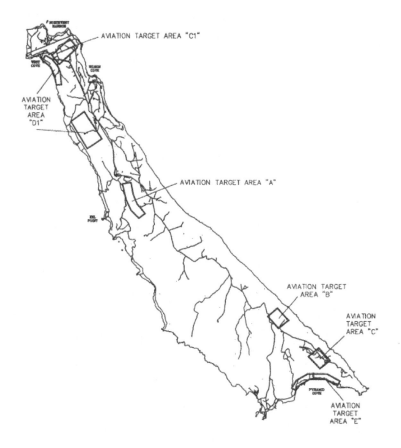

San Clemente Island was used as a practice landing area for the Marines. These were conducted to train the Landing Ships and the Marines in amphibious landings. The LSM convoy took an almost due west trip and arrived at the southernmost tip of San Clemente Island. Their destination was the Shore Bombardment Area (SHOBA) located at Pyramid Cove that was used for amphibious landing training and ship-to-shore target firing.

As we approached, I had received semaphore signal from the LSM-141, who was two hundred yards to our bow. He had relayed to me a message that originated from the lead ship, the

LSM-236. The ship's signalman waved both flags in the up position in my direction waiting on me to respond. Before he could continue, I held my left flag over my knees and the right flag in the up position indicating that I was ready to receive the message. He commenced to display each signal as I translated. In between each word, he held both flags in front of his knees indicating *"end of word"*. This went on until he gave his last word as *"AR"* which indicated *"end of message"*. His message read that all ships were to assume positions abreast at two hundred yards apart when approaching the shore. With both flags in hand and arms extended out to both sides, I answered with the signal for "*R*" indicating that his message had been received and understood.

Then, all at the same moment, we all turned to starboard and roared to the shore. When we had reached a distance of eight hundred twenty feet, we let go our stern anchor. Our orders were to practice dropping our cargo of tanks and platoon of Marines at the area of Pyramid Cove designated as Green Beach. Then, we were to reload the same tanks and Marines and do it again. Each time, we did this our time was a little better. With bullets blazing in combat, every second counts and we had to get on and off those beaches as quickly as possible. Most of the time we could do it in under five minutes. As we made landings, we would adjust just how far out we had to let go the anchor. The second time we landed with the same Marines, we tried the anchor at four hundred fifty feet. We used that "magic" number on all our landings at Pyramid Cove. That DID work better at Pyramid Cove, but, several factors influence beach landing, and that was the intentions of the practice. We would learn that when we got to Iwo. Every beach would be different. Every landing would be different.

We had been commissioned the same day back in June as the LSM-142 and here we were thousands of miles away from that dock practicing for war together. After we had made the landings at Pyramid Cove, we had paired off to carry out towing, fueling and passing the mail exercises.

26 September found us back at the Marine Base on White Beach. We disembarked the Marines, along with the tanks we had practiced with before. We took on five different M4A1 tanks and twenty new Marines and two officers for the next practice run. We practiced with this group for the remainder of the day and night. We ran through general quarters drills with the Marines in fire drills, man overboard drills, and abandon ship drills.

At noon the next day, we took formation with the other three ships in our practicing convoy to Green Beach at Pyramid Cove. The two hundred three foot vessels fanned out four abreast approaching the shore, and all trailed out the stern anchor five hundred feet out. The gray metal amphibian slid across the sand, opened the bow door, and lowered the ramp. The Shermans roared to life, lurched into gear, and their metal tracks clanked along the steel deck floor making a sound much like a crab across a dock, and then silenced as the tracks met the moist sand. With the well deck bare again, we raised ramp and closed doors, and retracted from the beach to circle back out to open ocean. We circled for about forty-five minutes to allow the Marines to carry out a beach exercise of their own. When the orders came, we rendezvoused to Green Beach to reload the same cargo and do it all over again.

We practiced those same orders the following day many times over. We practiced like a basketball team. We ran our plays and drilled through possible scenarios to make sure we could beat the opponent we had to face in the game. Except this was no game, and we knew it. The Nips played for keeps. There were no time-outs, and players who were substituted for rarely went back in. When this practice was complete, we were ordered to leave the Marines at Green Beach this time. The Marines were staying on San Clemente to practice, and we were going back to the Marine base to pick up more. Every time we went back we picked up more men and more equipment. This time we picked up twenty-two men and six tanks. Our convoy also grew from four amphibians to eleven.

On 2 October, we were ordered to assist the USS LCI-1026 off Green Beach. An LCI (Landing Craft, Infantry) is a one hundred fifty-eight foot vessel that is capable of landing up to two hundred personnel on a beach at one time. Apparently, the LCI-1026 had gone astern sideways onto the beach. It was forty-five feet shorter than an LSM and about half the displacement, but it was still a heavy whale when it was beached sideways. As we approached the beached LCI, I noticed the flag upon their mast as the Zebra (*We require a tug*). I immediately signaled back by semaphore that we were anchoring to their stern, and that we were going to try to get a line to them for a tow. The LCI's signalman waved his affirmative answer.

General Quarters!

At 1300 hours, our first attempt was to drop anchor just astern of the vessel and pass a cable to the LCI. We never could get the cable to the crew. I signaled to the ship that we were going to beach to their stern, and get a line to them that way. We then weighed anchor and beached westward of the ship, and were able get a line to the stern. Our idea was to pull the stern back out into the water to align the craft so that it could withdraw on its own. We backed from the beach and turned to gently pull the line taut. Immediately, we went to half, two- thirds, then full ahead. It wouldn't budge. We were then ordered to anchor and wait for the flood tide which should occur at approximately 1700 hours. Sure enough, by 1740 hours, with the aid of the tide, we pulled the stern around and detached line from the LCI. Just moments later, the LCI-1026 retracted under its own power.

This was another invaluable lesson for all the landing craft. Getting sideways was not just an inconvenience, it could be deadly. A beached ship showing its broadside was a sitting duck for enemy artillery to blow the ship apart. We understood there was more to be concerned about than just the welfare of the ship. We had to consider the cargo and the Marines on board. Not to mention in a combat situation, there wasn't always time or the convenience to call for a tow. We had to get this landing thing to perfection, NOW, while we were on friendly beaches. That's what we did.

3 October found us delivering one Sherman tank to the Marines who were stationed on San Clemente Island for training maneuvers. We embarked the tank from White Beach and were immediately underway to Green Beach in Pyramid Cove. Ensign Nasset was the OOD for most of the last two days and had taken us through the landing of the tank and a mandatory gas mask drill. We didn't know if the Japanese were using the mustard gas much like the Germans had in World War I, but we had to be ready if they were.

After we had secured from gas mask drills, Lieutenant White left for a conference aboard the LSM-236 to discuss lessons learned and plans for upcoming training maneuvers which our LSM group would be involved. When he left, Ensign Nasset found it fitting that we had a well-deserved "swimming party" coming to us, plus I think he realized we had some "lax time" in the orders as well. The junior officers were more sensitive to our need to blow off steam than the captain. This was a pretty good way to do it if we couldn't get leave, and were less likely to get in trouble.

We had been used to the salt water by now because we would take a bath from time to time in the sea water that had accumulated down into the well deck. We called that our swimming pool. The bow doors were not water tight, they just came together reasonably enough to prevent flooding. The water would be in the well deck, and we could stand in the bottom. You couldn't literally swim in it, but you could bathe in it or just wade around. We would do this when we were not under general quarters or in a war zone. We had a duty station so we usually had to take showers at the appropriate times.

We were anchored out in about fourteen fathoms of water just off the coast of Pyramid Cove beach. George Cimbala was our signalman on duty while it was my turn to swim and he helped keep a lookout for the sharks. We would have guys with rifles to help George lookout while the rest of us would dive off and swim. This particular time, it was Harvey Hobert (*radarman*) and "Doc" Mallchok who stood lookout on each side of the bow. They were a couple of the self-proclaimed "best shots" on the ship along with me. The three of us had grown close because we all shared the same interest in deer hunting back home. We felt pretty good about having them because we all knew they wouldn't miss if anything nasty was spotted in the water. The water was relatively calm that day, so it made it easier to see sharks. But, you never know about a shark.

We opened the bow doors where there were ladders built in, and lowered the ramp into the water. We climbed up the ladder of the bow door which was a good twenty feet, walked out to the end of the door, and dived into the ocean. Then, the boys could pull themselves up on to the end of the ramp, and do it all over again. We had a lot of fun. It's really comical to watch a bunch of teenage sailors in their skivvies, or some stark naked, jumping into the ocean. I didn't want anyone back home to get the word that I had been a savage and just jumped off in the buff, so I wore my skivvies.   When it was my turn to jump, I always gave it a good look because I had realized that the ocean animals could be a little more dangerous than the ones I was used to off the shores of Ludington.

Frank Swartz was the first in the water because he wanted to show off his diving skills that he had honed as a boy while cliff diving in Washington state. He had also trained for the Olympics for several years until the war came along and put those plans on hold. He was really good. He kept his body straight and rigid, then leapt from the doors into a double somersault. Just before he met the water, he straightened his torso into a perfect dive with almost no splash. None of it was bull. He was really that good. Well, when he surfaced, he climbed upon the ramp wearing nothing but a smile. His dive was a little too good. When he straightened his body, his skivvies slid right off. We saw them surface, but the waves carried them out to open sea. He didn't even try to retrieve them.

We had a couple of boys who came up next, Verlin Smith and Bill Schorer. Verlin was completely nuts so he was always trying to entertain us with his shenanigans.   He and Bill decided they would just do a double cannonball off each door at the same time. They hit the water with an enormous splash, and we all had to grade the height of the radial jets. They were achieving ten footers. If this was an Olympic sport, they would have been the best. About that time, George Cimbala yelled from the conn,

"Shark!"

Harvey and Doc scanned the water with their rifles as Bill and Verlin made a bee line for the ship. They just about killed themselves getting to the ramp; Bill got a pretty good bruise on his shin as he hurdled aboard. They both turned to see that the dorsal fin hump to the surface and descend once again. Bill could tell by the curvature of its back that the "killer" in the water was a Common Dolphin. When he came to the realization that he wasn't going to get eaten, he flipped his lid:

"George, you knucklehead! It's a dolphin! Can't you tell the difference? I oughta belt you right in the mug!"

"Sorry Bill. I thought you were done for." George retorted.

Harvey Hobert stood straight, grinned, and casually shoulders his rifle as he interjected,

"George just wanted to see how quick you could move. Anyway, girls go for wounded sailors. You can hobble around next time you're on liberty, and the dames will come runnin'"

"Yeah! Well, you're a real hoot Harvey! Wise guy!"

When we had some time, we had to do our own laundry. There wasn't anyone who did it for us. It was every man for himself. Well, once we were underway from the "swimming party", I took care of some my dirty "rags". There was a big washer on board we could all use. Of course, with those stiff new blue jeans, we would tie a line to them and throw them over the stern. Our screws would throw up a froth that would clean them in just a few minutes. Unfortunately, the first time I tried that, all I pulled in a half an hour later was the few threads that were left.

***

On our way back to our berth at Pyramid Cove on 20 October, we developed an extremely distressing vibration that was coming from the stern. It felt like the bottom was going to come out from under us. Ensign Bryan had taken all he could so he called condition Mike and we anchored in place. We reported the issue, and were ordered to the Harbor Boat Company Dry Dock at Terminal Island. Tug #T061 arrived at 1425 hours, connected the lines and towed the 143 to the dry dock. We were never sure what had caused the problem, but we suspected it was sustained during one of the landings. Ensign Bryan speculated that we had scraped along a reef and didn't realize it at the time. We arrived at Terminal Island two hours later and were taken into the dry dock. All the water was pumped from the dock and we were secured onto the cradle. Yard workers came aboard to assess the damage and began work on the propeller shafts.

By 0700 hours, 23 October, three days later, the dry dock commenced flooding and we were afloat once again. As soon as muster roll was taken, we manned our stations and got underway for our berthing area and some "R and R". The LSM-143 was alive and kicking once more.

We moored at Berth 230 C, Terminal Island for two days of well-deserved liberty that we all had coming. Many of the boys had painted the town, but Harvey Hobert always painted it a little too red. We were all called to muster at 0800 hours on 25 October as always, and once again, Harvey was AOL. Lieutenant White was livid. When the captain held mast the next day, Hobert lost the privilege of his subsequent liberty and given eighteen hours extra duty. I would have thought that Harvey would have learned his lesson when he got into that fight with John Lurding back at Little Creek. He escaped Captain's Mast that time, but he had pushed his luck a few times with the captain ever since. Harvey was our radarman and a good sailor there was no doubt about that. Even if he was late on board, we could count on him when we were underway, and he did his duty just like the rest of us. It's just that liberty was always difficult from him to handle. However, as Navy men we had to learn how to handle ourselves in all situations. I believe that most of our boys got the idea and began to straighten up. I was already responsible when I was at home in Fountain. I had to learn at an early age that other people count on you. I had to work the farm with my Grandpa and help him with his carpenter work and the mechanics on that old Model T. When it came to combat, we wouldn't have the luxury of waiting on people we couldn't count on. You have to work as one unit. If our duty slipped, then three or four others down the line would too. As time went along, muster call was one hundred percent every time. I think since Harvey and I were friends, he knew that I didn't approve of his actions. I think he realized, like we all did, that we represent the LSM-143; well heck, we represent the Navy. When it was all said and done, we represented it well.

***

We made preparations in accordance with orders received by our commanding officer to supply the LSM-143 and make final repairs and alterations for our voyage across the Pacific. The engine room telegraph had to be repaired and upgraded, and we had to replenish our ammunition stock. We changed our berth to 230 D-E, Terminal Island, California on 29 October to take on ammunition stores. At 1900 hours, I hoisted "Baker", and we began to take aboard the munitions. We received 5940 rounds of 20mm AA HET, 2880 rounds of 20mm AA HEI, 272 rounds of 20mm AA TAR, 20mm ready magazines loaded, twenty-six rounds of 40mm TAR, 1536 rounds of 40mm HET, 2000 rounds of .22 caliber ball long rifle, two hundred rounds .30 caliber ball, five hundred twenty-six rounds of .45 caliber ball, sixty Very pistol cartridges, and one Mark 2 smoke and one Mark 2 green smoke.

The first day of November found us still on the coast of the United States and rendering preparations in order to make way to the Hawaiian Islands. We moored at Berth 97 at the

Standard Oil Fueling Dock in San Pedro and took on 38,571 gallons of diesel fuel. Then, at 1450 hours, the tug YTL-488 shifted our berth to #92 where we were to undergo deperming of our ship's hull. While docked at the deperming facility, we received PhibTraPac (Amphibious Training Pacific) Secret Dispatch #282358 ordering us to our final stateside destination before steaming across the Pacific to Hawaii.

Doc Mallchok inspected our food supplies that came aboard on the morning of 5 November. We received enough fresh food to fill the reefer for the trip to Pearl Harbor. These stores included: dozens of eggs, hundreds of pounds of beef, ham, sausage, chicken, butter, cheese, beans, coffee, spaghetti and sauce, sugar, and flour. Among the food supplies were items to prepare for the Christmas "feast" we would undoubtedly be bestowed when that day arrived. These included: forty-eight packages of fruit cake mix, forty-six pounds of nuts, and one hundred fifty six cans of cranberry sauce. We also received cartons of cigars and cigarettes to further lifelong habits of smoking for some of the guys on board including myself. Lucky Strikes were the serviceman's best friend during war. It gave comfort and aided in calming the nerves; at least that's what we were told. War was a good advertisement for Lucky Strike. It kept us young men addicted for years after we left the military. That would be a habit I wouldn't be able to kick until the late-1960's. And, I'm glad that I did.

Six men reported on board for duty with transfer papers and sea bags to include: George Coyle, S2c; Basil Overton, F2c; Thomas Young, F2c; Curt Cummings, F2c; Clarence Phy, S1c; and Rex Baker, S1c. Along with the men, we received one frequency meter, a LM-13 battery, and fifty assorted radio tubes in case of malfunctions in the radio room.

We were sent across the bay from San Francisco to Oakland to the Naval Supply Depot to take on GSK (Glaxo Smith Kline) materials. These materials, we would discover, were power poles dripping with creosote. It was a stinking mess, and our well deck was now full of this stuff. It smelled so bad that we couldn't sleep. The odor was drawn into our sleeping quarters by the ventilation that was designed to supply us with fresh air. There wasn't anything fresh about that air. It was putrid and it stung our sinuses and lungs. I was even glad to be topside on duty rather than try to go below and sleep. I had the best seat in the house for fresh air up on the conn, and that is where I tried to stay as much as possible until we got to Pearl. I could be alone with my thoughts. Sometimes that was good; sometimes that was bad. An idle mind tends to wander and long for the things that a sailor is not supposed to dwell upon, but reliving precious memories could also help us continue onward.

6 November 1944 would mark the day that we left the American mainland to face an enemy we had only heard about. We had only fought in simulations on islands against an enemy

that didn't fire back. We had practiced the landings and emergency drills to perfection. Would we be that efficient when push came to shove? Were we ready for the ferocity of the Japanese? Eighteen year old sailors and Marines didn't worry about it. We were ready to take the war to the Japs. I wondered how many of those boys would see the mainland again; I wondered if I would. With the law of averages, I knew we all wouldn't make it back. We had heard of the battles of Tarawa, Saipan, Guam, and scanned the causality lists for friends and loved ones. I couldn't help but wonder what the people back home would say if my name was on that list. Would I be just another number to fade away into history like so many before me? When I saw a name on the list, I imagined that his mother and father grieved for days while they waited for any details. I imagined a girlfriend waiting for a reply to fifteen of her letters only to be mortified to find his name among the alphabetical register.

As we approached the Golden Gate Bridge, I glanced up at it for what I thought might be my last time. Most of the crew was topside to bid farewell to our beloved country. We might have been hokey or a little naïve, but we were all patriotic. We were willing to lay it all down to protect our land, our families, our loved ones. Then, I heard George Cimbala yell from the stern:

"Golden Gate in '48!"

Doc Mallchok, the constant optimist replied:

"Back alive in '45!"

I yelled down from the conn:

"Out of the sticks in '46!"

Verlin Smith peered up at me theatrically with his arms unfurled like a vicar during a Sunday service and countered:

"From Hell to Heaven in '47!"

We all had a good laugh, and the boys shared small talk as they leaned against the rails and nostalgically peered back at the mainland. I had heard those phrases back and forth between guys in a bar or some other occasion when the mood became nostalgic. From the conn, I stared back at San Francisco Bay with the sun up in its 1000 hours position; hovering over us in its warm reassurance. I had to wonder which one of those boys was right. Would this terrible conflict wage on another two or three years? Would the Japanese ever give up? I wanted to see the Golden Gate again, but I didn't want to wait until 1948. I said a silent "goodbye" to the Golden Gate Bridge and my family I left back in Fountain, Michigan. I looked upward at the magnificent, azure sky painted with puffs of hovering altocumulus clouds. I closed my eyes, breathed in the sweet, warm, Pacific breeze, and then prayed for the Pacific Fleet. I couldn't just request His protective hand over us and our safety. I knew to ask that was too much in a time of war. So instead, I asked God for what I had learned to ask for when times seemed dire; that His WILL be done.

Chapter 7

THE ENDLESS EXPANSE

The Pacific: the largest body of water on Earth. It extends from the Arctic Ocean in the north down to the Southern Ocean near Antarctica in the south. It is bound by Asia and Australia in the west and the American continents in the east. It owns forty-six percent of the Earth's water surface, and one-third of Earth's total surface area, making it larger than all of Earth's land area combined. Aboard the LSM-143, we had no idea the expanse that this body of water actually entailed. We would soon find out at a maximum speed of thirteen knots.

At 1022 hours, 6 November, 1944, we were underway in obedience to the Amphibious Pacific Fleet dispatch for Pearl Harbor, Territory Hawaii. Leaving San Francisco, the LSM-143 with her well deck loaded with creosoted pilings and one small craft set a course for Pearl Harbor. We had taken our position at the end of a column astern the LSM-264, LSM-142, LSM-261, and the LSM-141 respectively, as we all passed through the submarine nets at the entrance of San Francisco Bay. We were making various speeds to stay with the column with orders to rendezvous with convoy SP17 once we reached open ocean.

We passed East Farallon Island just abeam to starboard at a

distance of about two miles. Just as we cleared the island, I saw this ominous figure appear and a knifing dorsal fin slice the surface. It was making a beeline to the coast of that little island chain. As enormous as this creature was, it had to be a Great White. We had been told that elephant seals populated the Farallon Islands and fell victim to the Great White quite often. It was even a tourist attraction for many years. In recent years, some individual sharks had been tagged and found to roam the Pacific as far as Hawaii, returning regularly to the Farallones every year in the autumn.

Fifteen minutes after passing the East Farallon Island, our LSM column broke formation to take our proper convoy positions with engines ahead flank to catch the larger ships of the fleet. We had taken our position as the third ship astern the USS Alkes (AK-110) and the USS John I Nolan at a distance of seven hundred yards with our engines ahead at two-thirds. We were all part of a sixteen ship convoy that was a cadre of vessels including LSMs, AKAs, destroyer escorts, and troop ships. The USS Alkes was a cargo ship with Shermans, LCVP, artillery, trucks, jeeps, flamethrower fuel aboard enroute to Hawaii and the Marshall Islands for delivery. The USS John I Nolan was a liberty ship with a hull full of Marines most of them replacements and others on their way back to duty in the Pacific.

We had performed our exercise drills as always along the

way to Pearl. We exercised in fire, man overboard, and general quarters where all hands manned their battle stations in mock battles. No rounds were fired, but it was a full dress rehearsal. These drills became more random, I presume to make sure we were on our toes. We could have performed these tasks in our sleep as much as we practiced them. In all military training, it is doing the simplest tasks over and over again that makes the individual respond automatically without thinking. It is this automatic response that can save one's life or the lives of the boys on board.

One of the sailors that had come aboard while we were taking on supplies and the telephone poles was Basil Overton. He was a titan of a boy at about six foot four and two hundred twenty-five pounds. He had worked on his family's farm growing tobacco and raising pigs and cattle. All that southern hard work had chiseled his physique to more like a football player than what I pictured a down home farm boy would look like. His dialect was new to me because I had never been around southern people. His deep-voiced southern drawl was pleasant when he would describe life back home. The closest thing Basil had experienced to compare to an ocean in Perry County was the Buffalo River; the largest tributary of the Duck River in Lobelville, Tennessee. There were many catfish in the Buffalo that Basil would catch by way of a trot or limb line. These passive methods of fishing involved tying a line to an overreaching branch and a bated hook which was dropped down into the water. The line would be weighted in order to reach the desired depth for snagging the catfish. Unfortunately, the largest aquatic animal often found in the Buffalo was the alligator snapping turtle, which was often caught on trot and limb lines. It was just a necessary obstacle that had to be overcome when Basil would go after the succulent prize of the catfish. On the days he wasn't doing chores on the farm, Basil could be found rowing up and down the river in his flat bottom boat checking his lines. He would row along smacking mosquitos from his arms that frequented the warm evening air that he breathed in with youthful relish. He would share these memories time and time again filling the endless days of boredom with his fishing techniques.

Basil was a fireman (F2c) and he appeared to be at home on the Pacific while tending to his duties during the drills. I'm sure the reason he was chosen for the F2c position was his unusual size. He could manhandle the hefty water hoses and get them attached to the manifolds in record time. However, he confided in me since he arrived on our ship in Oakland about his fight with seasickness. He explained to me that it happened almost every day during training. The pitch and yaw of the LSM way overshadowed the calm flow of the Buffalo River in Tennessee. He spoke of taking Dramamine for the seasickness almost every day as he would lean over the side and expel every chunk of breakfast he had that morning. This display would delight the boys who had lived near the ocean and had been used to rides out in the waves. However, Basil would soon become a seasoned sailor; an old salt of the sea. Nothing would bother him, and he exhibited every aspect of a true sailor. He presented an unwavering confidence and courage. On the other side of Basil was his southern charm and gentility. He was courteous and loyal, a good man to have at your side. We came from two different worlds, but in a short time, we became good friends.

After ten days at sea, at 0840, 16 November, we had spotted land just off the starboard bow. Once a day we set back the clock thirty minutes each time we passed into a new time zone, and by the time we spotted the island of Oahu on the 16th, we had done this at least five times.

We were estimated to be at a distance of about seventeen miles away from the Hawaiian Island of Oahu. The island was absolutely awe-inspiring. The turquoise water and the emerald landscape were beyond description. Off in the distance, the Wai'anae and the Ko'olau mountains rose to the sky in all of their majesty. It almost made us forget about the war. Almost. The palm trees danced in the warm breeze. I took a deep, satisfying breath of the warm air, and closed my eyes for a moment. I reopened them just in time to see a lone albatross glide above the deck, bank left, and dive like a F4U Corsair with a Zero in its sights. These magnificent birds followed us everywhere on the Pacific. They hardly ever flapped their wings, but instead glided using the wind and gravity to rise and dive while gracefully hunting for prey. This bird was so much in control of the wind and their path of flight that they expended almost no energy. Sailors were superstitious about the albatross. In the epic poem *Rime of the Ancient Mariner*, an albatross lead the ship out of the Antarctic waters, but the mariner killed the bird with his crossbow. As penance for his crime, the mariner had to wear the dead albatross around his neck as a sign of regret for killing the bird. Thus, the popular phrase *"albatross around one's neck"* refers to a heavy burden of guilt that one might possess. The poem also implied that an albatross carried with it the souls of drowned fisherman and sailors:

"At length did cross an albatross,

Through the fog it came;

As if it had been a Christian soul,

We hailed it in God's name."

I wondered if this magnificent bird that was guiding us into our first berth at Pearl Harbor would continue to guide us across this vast ocean and safely back home. Was it carrying the souls of the men who drowned in the hull of the Arizona on December 7, 1941? Not sharing the typical sailor's superstitious thoughts, I believed the albatross was a comforting sign from God that He would be watching over us. I believed those boys were there looking down on us and cheering us on our way to defeat this enemy who was trying to take over the Pacific. Maybe the albatross was the form our guardian angels had taken. I believe that many of our guardian angels came in the form of the sailors, pilots, Marines, and soldiers who were constantly around us, answering the call of duty.

We had orders from the Senior Officer Present Afloat (SOPA), who was aboard our lead ship the LSM-264, to leave the convoy formation and form in a column with the other LSMs. We took the same formation that we had left California; astern the LSM-264, LSM-142, LSM-261, and the LSM-141. We passed through the submarine nets at the entrance of Pearl and our column was directed into the West Loch by a small boat with hull number HP15. The six of us LSMs meandered through the channel until we reached our assigned berthing area referred to as Tare 9. I had noticed a brown, rusted looking object in the water to our port side. When it came closer into view, it was unmistakably a sunken ship. We had been told that the ships at Pearl Harbor had been cleaned up and most of the evidence of the Japanese attack was pretty much unnoticeable. To my astonishment, there was the bow of an LST jutting skyward from the water with the remainder of the vessel submerged. We idled on passed the wreckage and turned into our berthing area at Tare 9. The column of LSMs moored side by side at the Naval Ammunition Depot, West Loch, Pearl Harbor with our ship to the starboard side of the LSM-141.

We had asked around to different people in the area and couldn't find out any details about what had happened to the

half-sunken LST. It was a complete mystery until after the war when we learned about a disaster that had been kept under wraps by the military until the investigation was completed. The story we had heard after the war explained a lot to me about why the procedures for handling munitions had been ramped up from previous protocol.

During preparations for the landing at the invasion of Saipan, a catastrophic disaster occurred in the West Loch. Upon return from training maneuvers, several ships including LSTs were docked side by side to rearm and refuel. Orders were given to unload unneeded mortar shells from LST-353. The LST was also carrying scores of large drums full of high octane aviation fuel used for the refueling of amphibious tractors. The unloading job was carried out by untrained personnel who inadvertently dropped a box of mortar shells.

Photographs also show that many of the men were smoking near the fuel barrels even though they were told numerous times to refrain. The LST-353 erupted in a horrific explosion that sent flaming debris hundreds of feet into the air, raining down on other LSTs. LSTs tried to escape the carnage including the LST-69 that drifted just past the LST-480 who was helplessly hung up at its mooring posts. The LST-480 caught fire and began to burn out of control. An aft explosion caused the LST-480 to go down by the stern where it rested on the bottom with the bow the only section atop.

Firefighting boats struggled to gather the situation back into control, but the inferno just accelerated. Navy intelligence speculated the explosions to be acts of sabotage at first, and placed the area on high alert. The LST-353 drifted and finally sank near Tare 10 while the LST-39 burned and exploded as it drifted nearby.

The following week, Navy intelligence ruled against sabotage and stated that the explosion had been started by the dropping of the mortars aboard LST-353. Four days later salvage crews began their cleanup and disposal efforts of all the destroyed vessels. The lone vessel LST-480 was left in its final resting place on the southeast shore of Hanaloa Point at Tare 9.

***

During our stay at Pearl, we took on fresh water and a store of provisions for general mess from the Naval Supply Depot.

Small groups at a time were allowed into the town for twenty-four hours of liberty before leaving for the Marshall Islands on Sunday the nineteenth. Early that morning after muster call, we left the West Loch and moored at the fuel dock on the East Loch at 0930.

Later that afternoon, we made all preparations to pull out of Pearl Harbor on our next assignment. By 1500 hours, we received our secret dispatch orders to rendezvous to Eniwetok, Marshall Islands. We passed through the submarine nets at the entrance of the harbor before Ensign Juliana ordered the engines all ahead full. In our column of LSMs, the convoy steamed out into the open Pacific.

We had motored ahead full all night and into the next morning until 0807 when the rudder jammed at five degrees. The ship made a sudden turn and Ensign Juliana commenced steering from the after steering station on the bridge. All engines were ordered ahead standard while the problem was diagnosed. It was discovered that a switch controlling the indicator was turned off accidentally. Steering was commenced in the pilot house and the handles on the engine order telegraph were both dialed down to full once again.

The twenty-first found the LSMs testing their respective 20mm and 40mm guns. We fired almost forty rounds of 20mm and only two rounds on the 40mm at the towed target. With testing successful, we were secured from general quarters and back to our normal duties. Verlin Smith on his 40mm was always waiting for the opportunity to give *anybody* on board the business. He hollered at all the 20mm gunners with no person in particular.

"Heck boys! I don't think you hit anything! Do I need to throw some more 40s at it?"

On 22 November, we had tested the smoke screen generator aboard the ship. All LSMs employed a fogging machine that laid a screen in hopes to hide the troops from the enemy. The generator on the stern converted a special type of fog oil into a heavy white cloud of protective smoke which was useful in any screening operation. It could provide cover for demolition units working ashore or close in shore. It could additionally afford convoy or force protection particularly against enemy torpedo plane attacks. Finally, a fog screen could be employed to draw a curtain between the assault beach and the approaching boat waves to confuse and hinder enemy observation and fire control.

The next day, 1225 hours, Ensign Bryan and I were on the conn when I had sighted a vessel that was not part of our convoy. It was just part of my job to distinguish between US Navy vessels and non-Navy. I had gotten pretty sensitive to different shapes and nuances of our vessels after being around them during our training. Ensign Bryan pressed general quarters and announced:

"General quarters. General quarters.

All hands to battle stations. All hands to battle stations.
This is not a drill. Repeat. This is NOT a drill."

Every man rushed to his stations with all equipment and helmets on his head and of course, my helmet was always handy on the conn. Our boys manning the 20mm and 40mm guns had their feet nervously on the triggers. As the convoy came closer to the vessel, we had gotten word from the lead ship that it was two merchant ships. We were secured from general quarters and back to normal; whatever that was.

The International Date Line, 180 degree meridian was passed on Sunday, 26 November just passed midnight. And, in the next two days, we sighted the Aur Island and Kwajalein Island, both of the Marshall Island group. At 1032 on Wednesday, 29 November we sighted Eniwetok, Marshall Islands. With Ensign Merschel at the conn, we anchored in Area A, Berth Item 8 at 1325 hours.

Following muster roll on 2 December, we moored to the starboard side of the USS Beagle (IX-112), a four hundred forty-one foot Armadillo-Class oiler, from which we received 55,500 gallons of fuel for our move to Guam the following morning. At 0648 hours on 3 December, we received our secret dispatch with orders to proceed. By 0730 hours, we had joined our LSM column and the convoy was underway to the largest island on the Mariana Islands chain.

We exercised at general quarters on the way to Guam in fire drill, abandon ship, flooding drill, and along with all of these the flag hoist drill supported each. This was a drill in which all of the LSMs participated, and I was to communicate with the surrounding ships and translate their exercise signals. We performed various exercises until we reached the island of Guam on 8 December. Coincidentally, this was the third anniversary of the Japanese occupation of the island before being liberated by Allied forces on 21 July 1944.

***

Guam is the largest and southernmost island of the Mariana Island chain, and was the only U.S.-held island in the region before World War II. Guam was captured by Japanese forces on December 8, 1941, just hours after the attack on Pearl Harbor, and was occupied for over two and a half years. During the occupation, the indigenous people of Guam were subjected to acts that included forced labor, torture, beheadings, and rape, and were forced to adopt the Japanese culture. Over one thousand civilians died during the occupation of the Japanese.

It was not as heavily fortified as the other Mariana Islands, such as Saipan, that had been a Japanese possession since the end of World War I, but by 1944 it had a large Japanese garrison.

The Allied plan for the invasion of the Marianas, *Operation Forager*, called for heavy preliminary bombardment, first by carrier aircraft and planes based in the Marshall Islands to the east, then once air superiority was gained, close bombardment by battleships.

Then, on D-Day, 21 July 1944, the 3rd Marine Division landed on a beach just south of Agana and just north of the Orote Peninsula while the 77th Infantry Division landed just south of the Orote Peninsula. The first days of battle were slowed by fierce Japanese fire but by the twenty-ninth, the peninsula was secure. In a northward sweeping motion, the 3rd Marines took the left flank while the 77th Infantry took the right and pushed back counterattack after counterattack from the Japanese. By 10 August, all organized Japanese resistance had ceased. The Island of Guam was declared secured, and 21 July would be commemorated by the locals every year as Liberation Day. On January 24, 1972, a "straggler" Sergeant Shoichi Yokoi was discovered by hunters after surviving alone in a cave for twenty-seven years. He had never gotten news that the war was over.

***

By 1009 hours, 8 December, we were moored in Apra Harbor, Guam until we were ordered the following day to unload the poles we had been hauling around since we left Oakland. We beached on what was referred to as "Dock E" even though it was nothing more than the beach. We landed the ship as always except we didn't open the bow doors and lower the ramp. The poles we were hauling had to be off-loaded from the top by a crane. So, one at a time, these poles were hoisted off of the well deck with a crane and piled onto shore.

13 December found us underway to the Ulithi Islands which were an atoll of the Caroline Islands. We were ordered to deliver equipment that we had picked up from loading Dock J in Apra Harbor, Guam. We delivered our cargo to the Ulithi Islands on 15 December, and we had, once again, received our dispatch to make way to Kossol Passage, Palau Islands.

With the area of the Pacific we were about to cross certified to be infested with

Japanese submarine patrols, we were to travel in tandem with an escort ship and a cargo ship. The Japs were on the defensive and they were doing everything in their power to keep us from their beloved homeland. We were in accompany with the USS PC-589 and the USS Minnesotan. The PC-589 was fitted out as a "submarine chaser" and armed with one three-inch gun mount on the bow, one 40mm gun mount astern, and three 20mm guns mounted throughout. The stern was also equipped with two depth charge tracks and four depth charge projectors. Finally, the PC-589 was mounted with two "*Mousetrap*" Mark 20 anti-submarine rocket launchers. Each rocket launcher could propel a one hundred pound warhead up to two hundred eighty meters every three seconds. The craft was slightly smaller than our ship at one hundred seventy-five feet, but it could cruise at a speed of twenty knots.

By 1707 hours, on 16 December, we were underway to Kossol Passage with engines at two-thirds and Ulithi Island slowly shrinking from view. We were on alert the entire trip because of the submarine warning in the area. One of the counter measures that we incorporated in order to avoid the submarines was to use zig zag plans. Each plan had a number and took us around a different pattern at all engines two-thirds. We still practiced at general quarters with drills and firing of the guns at varying intervals. Using the zig zag patterns invariably made the trip take twice as long, but it was a necessary evil to keep from meeting the bottom of the Pacific and becoming a permanent fixture in Davy Jones' locker. The Japs were the holders of the key, but we weren't about to let them open the locker for us. Furthermore, with the fire power of our escort, the PC-589 held a bigger key and they were ready to shut the lid tight. This is reminiscent of an excerpt from the Navy fight song:

The Endless Expanse

Stand, Navy, out to sea, Fight our battle cry!

We'll never change our course,

So vicious foe steer shy-y-y-y!

Roll out the TNT, Anchors Aweigh!

Sail on to victory!

And sink their bones to Davy Jones, hooray!

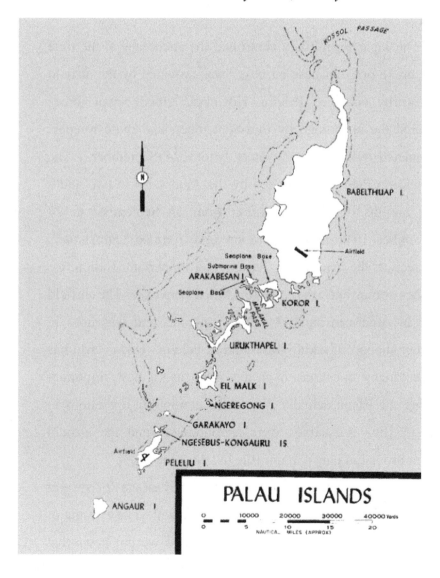

At 0634 hours, on Monday morning, 18 December, the Palau Island group came into sight. In particular we had sighted Kossol Passage. Kossol Passage was a large reef-enclosed anchorage at the north end of the Palau island chain. Both sides used it as a fleet anchorage during the war.

The Japanese initially controlled the anchorage at the time war broke out. Japanese air cover was provided by the airfield on nearby occupied Peleliu. However, Allied Naval forces secured the anchorage by mid-September, and minesweepers completed sweeping the waters before 24 September. The airfield on Peleliu was seized by the Americans in two and a half months of bloody fighting from 15 September to 27 November 1944 in an operation aptly termed *"Stalemate"*. Thereafter the anchorage became an important station for service forces and waypoint for Allied convoys. The airfield was in American hands by D-Day plus 2, and was used in further support of taking the island of Peleliu. However, it has raised many questions over the years as to how important taking the island actually was to the continuing operations in the Pacific. Casualties were astronomical, and the airfield never proved to play a major role in that respect.

We stayed at the anchorage at Kossol Passage for several days waiting for orders of our next assignment. The evening of Thursday, 21 December rolled around and we got news that some small boats would be coming to pick up the crew to see a movie on the LST-131 that was anchored just a few yards from us. That was the first time I had ever been on an LST, and we were taken down to the well deck where they had the projector and movie screen set up for the film. The well deck was huge compared to the LSM. It also differed from our open deck in that it had an upper deck with an elevator. The LST-131 was empty at the time, so there was plenty of room for both crews to watch the show. The picture we viewed that night was a John Wayne flick called *"The Fighting Seabees"* that was hot off the press just that year. It was another war movie, but it was still good to see John Wayne on the big screen to remind us of our theatre at home. Verlin Smith would go off on John Wayne every so often and he could do his voice just perfect. As always, we could count on Verlin to make light of everything. We finally got him to shush just so we could tell what was going on, but he would find scenes, especially with Susan Hayward, and make fun of the whole thing.

(Susan) Beautiful isn't it?

(John) Oh, it's you. Yes, it's pretty.

(Susan) Watching a ship's wake makes me think of the things that time puts behind us forever: Hopes; Dreams; Illusions. What does it make you think about?

(John) If they'd change the pitch of that propeller, we'd get a couple of more knots out of this tub.

(Susan) I thought I had caught you being human for once.

*Don't you have anything under that thick hide of yours
except cylinders and a carburetor?*

(John) A couple of spark plugs maybe...

Then, about the time they kissed on the deck overlooking
the ocean, all the sailors whooped and hollered and cheered
him on. A couple of guys gave John some suggestions about
his next move. We never really got to hear the whole movie
unless there were no love interests on screen. If it was a
serious drama, we did, but if there was the least bit of romance,
the boys made a fuss.

Verlin Smith yelled out,

*"Hey John! Ol' Bob is going to bust you in the kisser for
smoochin' his dame!"*

The whole deck howled with laughter as John Wayne left
Susan Hayward gazing off the deck.

A couple of hours later, we were picked up again by the
small boats and taken back to the 143 for our normal duties.
For the duration our stay in Kossol Passage, we moved from
anchorage to anchorage delivering and picking up cargo with
minesweepers, LSTs, cargo freighters (AF class), and so on.
We delivered drums of oil, various supplies, and equipment all
up and down Kossol Passage.

***

Christmas morning found us on deck at 0800 hours for
muster call. The deep orange sun peaked over the horizon and

sparkled its hypnotizing rays across the dancing wake in the distance. The waves painted each ray about its aquamarine canvas until the yellow-orange hue reached the side of the ship. The albatross bellowed his approval of the sun's majesty as he glided astern. With muster roll accomplished, we received the command *"Fall out!"* *"Fall out"* is used on ship instead of *"dismissed"* when the men were expected to stay close or proceed directly to their assigned posts. *"Dismissed"* was thought to imply that no further duty was required for an allotted period of time.

By 0900 hours thirteen other sailors and I were on a small boat to attend church services on the ARL-9 that was anchored in Berth 80. The ARL-9 was formerly LST-513 that had been refitted as an amphibious repair ship and was reclassified as ARL-9. Throughout the war, the ship was employed to make repairs at Kossol Passage, Leyte, and the invasion of Okinawa. It was reported that she continued repairs on damaged ships under the relentless suicide attempts by Kamikazes.

It was so surreal to be in the well deck of this ship and hearing all these sailor singing Christmas songs. The song I remember the most was Silent Night. I never realized what talented singers we had in the ranks. Hearing over one hundred men singing together is extraordinarily inspirational. I had attended a Christian service, but I know that there were other denominations being held on other ships. It was a great time to connect with God and fellowship with the other Navy boys.

General Quarters!

We knew when we got back on board our ship, it would be chow time. Compared to some of those guys on the beach, I was still thankful that I had a ship around me. We had people in the 'cook shack'; the galley; who cooked everything for us. They had huge ranges that they cooked the food on. The range must have been about 8 feet long and about 4 feet wide. We had tables set up in a forward crew compartment just off the well deck. We had to go down this unconventional ladder. It was actually steps with hand rails that were very steep leading us down to the galley. We would get in the line and our trays were filled with whatever was served as the meal of the day. We had three meals a day, but it wasn't as good as it sounded. Our stuff would get freezer rot. Things would be hanging in the freezer so long that it got spoiled. A lot of the things were spoiled. Flour especially would spoil. We used flour every day. We made pancakes out of flour. We didn't have pancake flour, we just had flour. The worms got in the flour. I mean, I'm not sure whether they got in it, or they were there all along. After a time, it just went bad. At first, when we would have pancakes, we would be busy picking worms out. After a while, it got so bad, we just ate it worms and all. If we picked out everything that was in the flour, we would have to throw the whole meal away. We also had turkey on every third Sunday. The turkeys and the chicken were no different. They were freezer burned, and they were just practically rotten. We ate it. We didn't have any choice. So these three hot meals a day

142

weren't all that they were cracked up to be. We were eating bread with worms and pancakes with worms. This was not by choice but they were cooked, baked, or fried right into the batter. They might have come under the heading of "protein". We did not have any K-rations or C-rations. We had something cooked. It was better than nothing, but not much. It was wartime. We didn't get re-supplied every week. It may have been every two or three months. A ship had to be moored near a base somewhere or be "cozy" with a big ship. We would go along side one of the big ships and get reprovisioned. There was no set time. Whenever the opportunity presented itself was when we were refurnished. Things from the big APA or AKA ships still weren't always as fresh as we would have liked.

We didn't have just regular milk or potatoes; it was instant where you had to add water. The potatoes had bugs and worms in it just like the flour, but like the flour, we ate it anyway. We had our own water distillery. Every ship of any size had provisions to purify its own water. We would just take sea water and the machine would extract the salt and purify the water. Then, we could drink it or make the food that needed water added. The cooks could hydrate the milk and make the potatoes with the purified sea water.

We came back on board the ship and Christmas dinner was cooking in the galley. It smelled different. It had a more of a Christmas flare to it. When we were all called to mess at 1200 hours, we were treated with a real spread. The ship's cooks, Harry Brown (*Ship's Cook Second Class – SC2c*) and Paul Lenzi (*SC3c*), really tried to make the most of what they had, and sometimes that was pretty lean. However, this time, we had a good, fresh supply of food. The menu consisted of roast turkey and dressing, mashed potatoes, buttered peas, creamed asparagus, sliced tomatoes, hot rolls, and cranberry sauce. For dessert, we had a choice of pumpkin and/or mince pie. They even had serving of hot coffee and lemonade. Of course, as always, there were cigarettes everywhere to finish it off. Ensign Merschel blessed the meal and prayed for our safety in the inevitable operations that laid ahead for us. He really put things into perspective. We were grateful for the wonderful meal, but we knew it wouldn't always be like that. We ate the meal with great fervor and levity of heart just like teenage boys would. We packed it away like it was our last meal while Verlin told jokes and quoted lines from the movie we just watched the night before on that LST. He was once again doing John Wayne's voice and changing the lines to make them a little funnier. We laughed and finished off the pie, started a few card games, and then listened to "Tokyo Rose" play Bing Crosby's "*White Christmas*" over the airways. In her best broken English, she spilled her propaganda:

"*Good evening my Yankee brothers. This is the voice of truth coming to you once again from the peaceful islands of*

Japan. This one goes out to all of you poor boys in the Pacific stuck on a nasty island or packed into a dusty ship. Don't you miss your family; your girlfriend? Don't worry. She is being very well taken care of by the boy that lives next door. He will take her to the theater to see that Cary Grant movie she has wanted to see. Not that they will actually watch the movie. Anyway, I know you are dreaming of a white Christmas. Maybe they are having a most joyful one without you in America. Enjoy."

Bing Crosby's wonderful baritone voice echoed over the loudspeaker as we all sat in somber foreboding in our own thoughts. Not one man uttered a word. We hung on with nostalgia to the homely song while ignoring the hoopla that she spewed over the radio. I told myself it was just hateful propaganda, but I still couldn't help wondering what was happening thousands of miles away in America. It was Verlin's turn to deal the cards for our four-player pinochle game, and he spun a card to each of us in uncharacteristic silence. It became hard to focus on the game as we clung to the carol's every word:

"I'm dreaming of a White Christmas;
Just like the ones I used to know..."

Chapter 8

SUICIDE SWIMMERS & HUMAN TORPEDOES

By 1800 hours Christmas Day, we were underway with orders to beach at Peleliu Island, Palau. We arrived on the southwest part of the island at Orange Beach, Peleliu early on

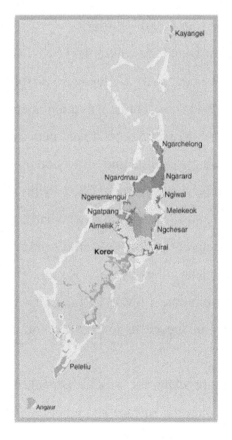

Wednesday morning, 27 December, and anchored in order to transfer twenty boxes of freight to the AGS-2. We were then ordered by the port director to proceed to the eastern side of the island to Purple Beach. There, we moored alongside the Liberty ship USS James Bonham to deliver cargo at 1400 hours.

We arrived off the coast of Angaur Island on the morning of New Year's Eve at around

0900 hours. We were only sent there for twenty-four hours to make a couple of ship to ship deliveries. We first moored to port side of the USS Daniel S Lamont, Liberty Merchant ship, and made our deliveries. Then, later that night at around 2000 hours, the USS Enos A. Mills arrived and we, once again, moored port side and offloaded needed supplies to the ship.

We had untied from the USS Enos A. Mills and were underway while awaiting further orders. We circled in the harbor near Cape Ngaramudel on the southwest coast near the phosphate plant that had been so important to the Japanese when they held the island just four months earlier.

The waters around Angaur Island are where the LSM-143's first encounter with the enemy occurred. A Japanese prisoner captured on Peleliu late in 1944 stated that he was a member of a "Kairyu" swimming unit with twenty-one other men each equipped with three grenades, a knife, and a wooden box measuring one hundred sixty cubic inches filled with the explosive Lyddite. They were surface swimmers who had been hastily trained to attack landing craft. Earlier in the war, such swimmers had been used to clear mines in Hong Kong. They were especially trained to obliterate LSMs, LSTs, LCIs; the larger landing ships that would be close to shore or on the shore. That included us!

The Japanese had a more elaborate suicide squad that would be even more deadly than the surface swimmers. They referred to those "frogmen" as Fukuryu or *crouching dragons*.

They were even sometimes laxly referred to as "human mines". Their equipment was a loosely fitting wet suit, a clumsy helmet much like a deep-sea diver, bulky air circulation device and purification tanks strapped to the chest and back, linked by a tangle of hoses. The training proved to be more suicidal than the actual missions which never materialized. There were many fatal accidents during the training because the twin-tank oxygen equipment did not allow for proper inhale and exhale invariably causing asphyxiation.

To destroy an inshore landing craft, each Fukuryu was armed with a twenty-two pound impact-fused charge, incorporating a floatation tank mounted on a pole. This was reminiscent of the anti-tank lunge mines utilized by the Japanese infantry. The diver would walk on the ocean floor or swim up to the landing craft, hopefully undetected, and drive the fuse into the hull immediately detonating the explosive. The war ended before the Fukuryu could be perfected for operational use.

The LSM-143 was enroute around Angaur Island, Palau. At 2300 hours on 31 December, two Japs were reported in the water. This encounter occurred one month after the bloody Battle of Peleliu had ended. Scuttlebutt had warned us that the Japanese were attaching bombs to the side of ships. Ships had to stay underway because it was too deep to anchor. I was tasked that night to scan the water with my spotlight to keep an eye out for these so-called "suicide swimmers". They would have a box, or something, with an explosive charge and the Japs would be in the water. They would just swim pushing this box full of explosives. Anyway, they were in a habit of pushing these explosive charges up against the sides of these ships that were underway. Well, it wasn't just scuttlebutt that time, it was the Real McCoy. The night was clear and cool as the gibbous moon reflected half of its light down onto the water's surface. The moon's outstretched reflection across the water did very little to aid in pinpointing foreign objects below. The water was calm, and I noticed how magnificent the stars were, twinkling above this eerie setting like a velvet blanket sprinkled with glitter. I had scanned the water back and forth for the last three hours since taking my post, and I only had one more hour until midnight when I would be relieved by George Cimbala. One of the most important jobs we had as a signalman was that of a lookout. We had to be observant and be sensitive to just the slightest changes in situations, and to be able to notice things that others would take for granted. It was a monotonous job, but I told myself that I had to stay sharp. I yawned in boredom, closing my eyes as my mouth outstretched to take in a breath. When I opened my eyes again, my senses were heightened as I fixated on a small object rising and falling against the waves in the distance. I had moved my light passed an entity figuring it was a dolphin or sunfish that had surfaced. I immediately trained the light back on the object.

This thing was about two hundred yards out on the starboard quarter, but I knew it was something on a float. There was no way that the float was moving toward us on its own. I could see it was a man, and it couldn't be anyone lost at sea. It had to be the enemy. I figured it was anyway. It had to be the explosives and a swimmer, or two, of which we had been alerted. I kept the light right on him, and notified Lieutenant Merschel. He leaned forward for a better look and squinted at the ominous figure in the distance.

"Are you sure it's Japs Garforth?"

"Well, I'm not positive, but it's definitely not a dolphin or a sunfish, Sir."

He gazed momentarily once more into the foggy distance, and then back to me.

"Sound general quarters!"

Following orders, I pressed the general quarters button. The orders echo over the intercom:

"General quarters! General quarters!

All hands to battle stations!

This is NOT a drill! Repeat! This is NOT a drill!"

The gun crews rushed to battle stations. The twin 20mm gun on the starboard side was referred to as Gun #5. The boys mounted the 20mm magazines on each barrel by leaning it slightly forward and pressing it downward with a click. Then, with the command from Lieutenant Merschel, the gun opened fire with a thirty round hail storm of lead. Both barrels spit tracers that blazed the way to the float and kept the gun on target. The tracers looked like fireflies on jet fuel reflecting their beams off the water's surface. The first fifteen or so rounds made a pitter-patter line straight to the float, then all of the sudden, an explosion erupted into the night sky. I mean it was a direct hit! I ducked my head behind the light momentarily, but I kept the light on the target. It had to have killed anyone or anything within one hundred yards of the explosion. We maneuvered the ship to stay with the target, but the smoke from the gun fire interfered with the searchlight and the target was lost.

"Cease fire!"

Lieutenant Merschel moved his head from side to side to try to avoid the smoke while he scanned the surface finding nothing left but the waves in the waters below. He congratulated the gun crew and me.

"Nice shootin', boys!"

Then, he turned to me and winked.

"Good eye, Garforth."

It's nice to be recognized for a job well done, but that WAS my job. I was the eyes and ears of the ship. It was part of the signalman's unwritten qualification. We had to be able to distinguish objects. I HAD to know an A6M Zero from an F4U Corsair; a Japanese ship from one of ours, a float from a fish.

When we were secured from general quarters, we joked and

called this our first battle. Verlin Smith roared with laughter and announced:

"There's your fireworks, boys! Happy New Year!"

***

By the end of 1944, the LSM-143 had logged 14,414 nautical miles. We literally ended the year with a bang. However, we knew the big bang was yet to come. The Pacific was teeming with dangerous creatures. The ones we were the most concerned about were the ones cruising above and below the surface inside bodies of steel.

***

By noon on New Year's Day 1945, we were underway for Orange Beach, Peleliu Island, making various courses and speeds to avoid submarine attack. By 1605 hours, we were lying off Orange Beach keeping clear of other ships awaiting orders to proceed to Kossol Passage for transport of supplies. I scanned over the island of Peleliu and found that it was an awful, cauterized mess. The trees, if they could be called "trees", were just black sticks with no leaves. There was just rock and coral everywhere. There was no vegetation left. The island was completely devoid of color that would indicate that any form of life existed. The Navy had blistered the entire beach with shelling, and left nothing but rubble and ruin in support of the Allied invasion in September 1944. I had read about the battle in newspapers, and was saddened by the number of Marines and soldiers we had lost to acquire the airfield on Peleliu. Our boys had to endure the three digit heat and the ferocity of the Japs hidden under ground.

By 2100 hours, we had received orders to proceed to Kossol Passage. We were accompanied by the USS Rotanin (AK-108) and escorted by the submarine chaser USS SC-1328. The USS Rotanin was a Crater-class cargo ship used to deliver troops, goods, and equipment to various war zones in the Pacific. We took our position abeam to starboard of the USS Rotanin, and both ships fell in astern to the USS SC-1328. The sub chaser had one 40mm mount, two .50 caliber machine guns, two depth charge projector "K Guns", two sets of Mark 20 Mousetrap rails with four 7.2 projectiles and two depth charge tracks. If there were any Japanese subs, the sub chaser would sniff them out and eliminate the menace.

We arrived at the entrance of Kossol Passage on 2 January at 0634 hours awaiting daylight to enter the anchorage through the submarine nets. Within the hour, we were in Berth 80 and let go the stern anchor to moor for the day. From that day to 13

January 1945, the LSM-143 kept either anchored or underway making deliveries and resupplying our stores. We spent most of our time at Kossol loading and unloading supplies and equipment from ship to ship and onto the shore of various landing beaches.

We also had time on our hands when we weren't at our stations. So, before I would leave my light, I would signal to a nearby LST or APA to ask if they had any new movies. On 6 January, I signaled the LST-131 to inquire about any flicks that they might have. They signaled back that they had several, and that they were also screening a show at 1800 hours in their well deck. The signalman invited any of our boys who were off duty to join their presentation. He also offered to send us a film for the sailors who had to stay on board. Sure enough, at 1845 hours they sent a small boat to pick up a party of twenty guys, and presented us with one that we could watch. That happened a lot. We usually didn't return the movie. It was understood that we would just send it forward to the next ship that wanted a movie. I never knew that I would have to also be the "entertainment director" of the ship when I was tasked as the signalman. The LST-131 hosted the last movie we had left the 143 to watch just last month. Since I was on duty and I had gone last time, I didn't go this time. We all covered for the other boys that didn't get to attend the last viewing. It was just kind of nice to get away for a while and check out another ship; to see how the other half lives.

General Quarters!

***

By mid-1944, the Japanese had suffered humiliatingly decisive defeats at Midway and the Marianas Islands. In undeniable desperation, Japanese military resulted to measures unimaginable just a few months before. In recognition of the unfavorable progress of the war, the Japanese high command considered suggestions for various suicide craft referred to as "*Toko*" or "*suicide weapon*". These were initially rejected, but later deemed necessary. Various suicide mission vehicles were developed in the *Japanese Special Attack Units*. For the Navy, this meant Kamikaze planes, Shinyo suicide boats, Kaiten submarines, and Fukuryu suicide divers or "*human mines*". The Kamikazes were somewhat successful, and the Imperial Japanese Navy harbored high hopes for the new "*Kaiten*" program.

The Imperial Japanese Navy called upon volunteers for a mission of unknown nature. It was explained by high command that this new weapon could inflict enormous damage upon the enemy and help to bring victory for their beloved Emperor and country. They were not told the exact nature of the mission until they arrived at a destination that they would only know as "*Base P*". Because of their navigational skills, these men were mainly taken from the class of Japanese Air Force pilots. As a result, the men who operated these new weapons were often signified as "*pilots*". Sekio Nishina volunteered to be one of the first men to take this secret weapon into battle.

Kaiten or *"human torpedo"* is literally translated in Japanese as *"return to the sky"*, *"the turn toward heaven"*, or commonly depicted as "heaven shaker". The names were appropriate as the pilots were promised that their reward for their mortal sacrifice was a special place in Heaven. Kaiten vessels were attached in groups of four to the top deck of fleet submarines of the Imperial Japanese Navy, and launched when they came within an acceptable distance to the intended target.

Research on the first Kaiten began in February 1944, followed on 25 July of the same year by the first prototype. By 1 August, an order for 100 units had been placed.

The very first Kaiten was nothing more than a forty-eight foot Type 93 torpedo modified with an engine compartment attached to a cylinder that would become the pilot's compartment with trimming ballast in place of the warhead and other electronics and hydraulics. It utilized a simple propeller engine driven by compressed air. The Kaiten's electric controls gave the pilot full reign of directing the watercraft into the target. However, the rudimentary, hand-cranked periscope gave the pilot his only view of his intended target. This made the vessel extremely difficult to maneuver around underwater obstacles and finding the intended target a daunting task especially in low light situations. Therefore, the missions had to be carried out during the day in order for the pilots to see where they were going. The pilot was cramped into a tiny cockpit located dead center in the vessel. The warhead and fuse was placed in the nose, and the fuel tank directly in front of the pilot. Not only would the detonation of the 1.6-ton explosive charge obliterate the pilot, but the fuel tank added an extra flammability factor to finish the job. That would send his body parts through the trim tanks and into the engine in the aft section. Most bombers in the Imperial Air Force carried only a quarter of the explosive power of the Kaiten submarine. The vessel, if successful, could singlehandedly sink any large warship including a battleship, cruiser, or the most coveted suicide pilot's prize; an aircraft carrier. It was originally intended for the pilot to guide the weapon close to the target, then eject out an escape hatch at the last minute. However, this was never utilized and the escape hatch was scrapped in any future developments. To render the detonation fool-proof, the Kaiten was fitted with a hand-held lever. On impact, the pilot is thrown forward triggering this backup detonator just in case the impact detonator failed. The lever was also designed in case the pilot made a miscalculation and had to detonate near the target instead of on impact. What had once been a simple torpedo was now transformed into a human-guided underwater missile.

The original designers and testers of this new weapon were Lieutenant Hiroshi Kuroki and Lieutenant Sekio Nishina. They were both to die at the controls of Kaitens. Lieutenant Kuroki met his death in a training accident testing a very early prototype. Nishina would meet his fate ramming his Kaiten into the first Allied ship struck by this new form of suicide weapon. Like the Fukuryu project, more men died in the training and development of the Kaiten program than in battle. In every aspect of Japanese suicide entities, death was thought to be the most honorable way to serve Emperor Hirohito.

The first successful Kaiten attack on an Allied vessel occurred in the early dawn hours on 20 November 1944. After emptying her fuel tanks into ships preparing for the landings at Leyte Gulf, the auxiliary oiler AO-59 named the USS Mississinewa set sail for the Allied anchorage near Ulithi. The sailors aboard the AO-59 referred to the vessel as *"the Mighty Miss"* or simply *"the Miss"*. This was used less as a term of endearment than that most sailors simply couldn't pronounce the name. Ulithi is an atoll in the Caroline Islands of the western Pacific Ocean whose lagoon served the US Navy with a perfect staging area for upcoming Allied operations. 16 November 1944 found the Mississinewa in anchor replenishing her stores of diesel fuel, fuel oil, and aviation gasoline in all tanks to full capacity. In the early morning hours of 20 November, the crew of the AO-59 was still asleep in their racks when the unimaginable occurred.

Captain Zenji Orita, commander of the Japanese submarine I-47, surveyed the over two hundred vessels anchored in Ulithi through his periscope. His plan was to deploy the four manned torpedoes attached to I-47 as close to the central part of the

Ulithi anchorage as he could without being detected. The sole surviving co-designer of the Kaiten, Lieutenant Sekio Nishina, was launched from the deck of the I-47 along with three other Kaiten vessels on their date with destiny.

Within just moments of release from the mother sub, two of the Kaiten run onto a reef. A third is erroneously identified as a midget sub and sunk by depth charges from an American destroyer. The lone remaining Kaiten is the one piloted by Sekio Nishina. Nishina's ultimate prize was an aircraft carrier, but he settled for the closest ship in his sights, the USS Mississinewa. Kaiten pilots had a much more difficult time aiming their suicide craft than their Kamikaze cousins in the sky. The only way Nishina could see the target was to crank a small periscope by hand leaving him vulnerable to enemy lookouts. He quickly decided a final bearing on the target. He cranked the periscope back down and slightly submerged under the waves. Once in range of the enemy, he disengaged the safety mechanism from the warhead. With his hand on the detonator lever Nishina began his high speed run. At the last moment, Nishina accelerated to high-speed toward the unsuspecting crew on the "Miss". The sailors onboard the Mississinewa are oblivious to the terror that is about to strike. At 0545 hours, the *"Heaven Shaker"* contacts the starboard hull igniting the warhead in its nose. The topped-off fuel tanks aboard the Navy oiler exploded as flames swept through the forward berthing compartments and through the open hatches.

Men were instantly killed in their racks. Flames leapt from the seventy-three foot hole in the hull. The choking smoke billowed over a mile into the sky as sailors throughout Ulithi on surrounding vessels looked on in horror. Witnesses close enough to the Mississinewa believed there was no chance for any survivors. The flames pursued the aft section as sailors began to abandon ship. They dived into an ocean mixed with thousands of gallons of burning oil and aviation fuel. Rescue boats from surrounding ships endured the fire and smoke to pull fellow seamen from the watery inferno. As a result of their courageous efforts, two hundred Mississinewa sailors are rescued from the oil and blazes. At 0700, the AO-59 lists to her port and completely capsizes. Then, within minutes the proud vessel sinks beneath the waves taking sixty-three men down with her.

The sinking of the Mississinewa would prove to be one of only two victories for the Kaiten. Less than half of the Kaiten pilots released from a mother submarine even saw their target. Over two thousand Japanese submariners carrying the Kaitens were lost by accidents or misfirings. The nominal success of the Kaiten was nothing more than a devastating failure for a program that bore such high expectations from the Japanese.

On 27 December 1944, the Japanese naval submarine group codenamed "Kongo" included submarines I-36, I-47, I-48, I-53, I-56, and I-58. They gathered to draw up plans that called for attacks on anchored American shipping at five different points. The attacks were to take place simultaneously on 12 January at widely-dispersed locations with I-class submarines laden with four Kaiten each. The I-36 was assigned Ulithi in the western Carolinas, the I-47 at Hollandia, New Guinea, the I-53 at Kossol Passage, the I-56 at the Admiralty Islands, and the I-58 at Apra Harbour, Guam. The I-48 was assigned to make a follow-up attack at Ulithi on 20 January.

Kossol Passage was an area that no one outside of a signalman, quartermaster, officer on deck, or a helmsman would have remembered. It was an ideal anchorage for our ships because it had an encircling reef that served as a natural barrier around the outside. This made it difficult for enemy ships and submarines to sneak into our area. It would completely rip the bottom out of a ship that wasn't aware of these reefs and knew where our secret opening was located. One had to know exactly where to enter and exit. We even had submarine nets across that opening. Any enemy sub would have tipped their hand if they tried to blow a hole through it and enter the anchorage.

Kaiten torpedo vessels were sighted in the waters at Kossol Passage on the evening of 12 January. Two were spotted in the area, and one was destroyed before the night was over. The only way that the Kaitens could have gotten passed the submarine nets, were to shadow an incoming ship before the nets could be closed.

Four miles off Kossol Roads, Palaus, at 0700, I-53 surfaced at the command of Lieutenant Commander Toyomasu. With considerable daring, I-53 penetrated the intensly patrolled entrances to Kossol Passage. When opportunity presented itself to Toyomasu's approval, the Kaitens were ordered to launch. The first Kaiten refused to budge from its launch pad. Then, when the crew was finally able to work it free, the commander was horrified at what he witnessed. This first Kaiten, piloted by Lt. Kuzumi Hiroshi, exploded just moments after launch due to a fractured fuel line. The number three Kaiten could not start its engine at all. Numbers two and four piloted by Ensign Ito Osamu and CPO Arimori Bunkichi were launched without incident. After an hour and twenty minutes, two explosions were heard by the captain of the I-53. The nearby 30th Base Unit confirmed two hits on Allied ships, and reported the erroneous news to the captain. I-53 surfaced to check out Kaiten number three to find that its pilot had lost consciousness due to fuel fumes.

An LST lookout had spotted one of the *"human torpedoes"*, and we tried to fire on it, but couldn't get our guns to depress far enough. If we were anywhere near close to hitting him, we were too close to lower our three inch .50 caliber gun. So, the captain made the order for us to make some circles that were big enough to stay out of the way of the Kaiten. As the ship made these fast circles, we began to lean in the direction of our intended target. When the ship achieved the desired angle toward the target, we'd fire the port guns. We could lean to the point to where the guns would depress just far enough. We fired a few rounds to no avail. We were then ordered to cease fire in order to not fire upon our own ships.

Just to our port side, the USS Captivate (AM-156) weighed anchor from its berth and sped at flank speed to investigate our gun fire. Immediately, the Captivate had the Kaiten in its sights and opened fire with its hedgehog rockets. The first three rockets splashed through the surface of the water with no success. Then, all of the sudden an explosion erupted from the depths that was confirmed later as a direct hit on one of the Kaitens that had breached the submarine nets that day.

We had no confirmation of what happened to the second human torpedo. They were not known to try to escape, but there was no second explosion that anyone in the anchorage had reported. None of our ships were hit by the Kaiten as the Japanese base had told the captain of the I-53. I knew that the suicide pilot didn't want to go back and explain that he didn't complete his mission and bring any shame to his family. We never found out what happened to the other Japanese suicide vessel. My best guess is that the two explosions were caused by the desperate pilots pressing the backup detonator near what they thought was an American ship. But, the main reason was that the Kaiten pilots knew that it would be disgraceful to return to the mother sub without completing their hopeless mission. With all Japanese suicide volunteers, the motto was absolutely *"death before dishonor"*.

***

We received our orders back to Guam on 13 January. During the month of January, the 143 operated as a cargo hauler between the sister islands of Guam, Tinian and Tanapag Harbor, Saipan and racked up 1,075 nautical miles.

We sighted Guam at 1033 hours on the sixteenth, and when we anchored at Apra Harbor, I surveyed the state of the beach. As I reflect on the conditions of many of the islands at that time, they had been invaded and neutralized by the Navy bombardment in case there were Japanese. The islands were practically eliminated. There was not a tree standing. All the palm trees had been blown down; all the shrubbery had been burned. It was just a piece of real estate. There was nothing pretty about any of those islands, at the time, because they had been shelled, strafed, and bombed to chase out the Japanese. The Navy would soften them up when Marines were going to invade the island. They were shelled some more; bombed some more. There was nothing standing, nothing good-looking, and nothing pretty about any of them. We weren't much into the scenery at the time but, man, when I saw those islands that had been completely annihilated like this one had been, I just got a sick feeling in my stomach. I thought back to Pyramid Cove, Barro Colorado Island, the Coiba Islands, and, of course, the Ludington breakwater, and just the absolute magnificence they possessed. I knew these islands had that splendor once before the war. It was so disheartening to see them reduced to charred ruins. I knew that once we rooted out the Japs, and we went home, God would restore those islands back to the beauty that war had destroyed.

***

Tinian Island was home to the Mine Assembly Depot #4 which was utilized in the preparation of ordinances for *Operation Starvation.* Operation Starvation was an American campaign to starve Japan into surrender by dropping mines from B-29s into the narrow entrances to the Inland Sea and off Japanese ports. The mines were to be specifically placed on the east coast of Japan in the Inland Sea lying between the main island of Honshu, Kyushu to the south, Shikoku to the

east of Honshu, and Korea.

As an island nation dependent on outside sources of oil, coal, raw materials, and foodstuffs, Japan was uniquely vulnerable to sea mine warfare. Operation Starvation proposed to bring Japan to its knees by cutting off all essential supplies from the outside world by laying mine fields in water routes and off Japanese seaports. An opportune result was that the operation also prevented Japan from provisioning its overseas military outposts.

The operation was conceived by Admiral Chester Nimitz, commander-in-chief of the U.S. Pacific Fleet and also commander of Allied forces in the Pacific. It was executed by Major General Curtis LeMay's 313th Bombardment Wing of XXI Bomber Command. It was to be carried out by roughly one hundred sixty specially adapted land-based B-29 Superfortresses flying night, low-altitude radar-mining missions and, to a lesser extent, by mine-laying submarines.

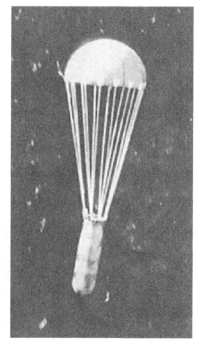

Unglamorous, inconspicuous, and inevitably overshadowed by the detonation of two atomic bombs in August 1945, Operation Starvation was one of the great unacknowledged successes of World War II. Operating from newly captured bases in the Mariana Islands (Tinian, Saipan, and Guam), the

XXI Bomber Command flew 1,529 sorties and laid 12,135 mines in twenty-six fields on forty-six separate missions. A total of six hundred seventy ships was sunk or damaged, accounting for more than one and a quarter million shipping tons. Traffic in most of the main shipping lanes was halted, delayed, or diverted and Japan's ports were left unusable. By August 1945 shipping had fallen to only one-quarter of May levels; already dangerously low, and Japan's economic collapse was all but inevitable.

Many historians argue that had it been introduced earlier in the war, it may have achieved Japan's uncondi-tional surrender without the bombing of Hiroshima and  Nagasaki. However, with the Japanese occupation of islands near their mainland and the logistical range of B-29s making it safely to and from aircraft carriers or land bases, it was not a feasible operation until the Americans gained control of the Marianas.

Aerial mining demanded less than six percent of the

XXI Bomber Command's total sorties, and only fifteen B-29s were lost in the effort. In terms of damage per unit of cost, Operation Starvation surpassed the U.S. Navy's anti-shipping submarine campaign and the USAAF's strategic bombing of Japanese oil production facilities and urban, commercial, and manufacturing centers.

We had received orders to pick up fifteen mine specialists who needed to be transferred from Guam to the Mine Assembly Depot #4. Their task was to assemble mines for *Operation Starvation* that would begin dropping these mines beginning 27 March 1945. We beached at the LST Landing area in Apra Harbor and began taking on the Navy Minemen and their equipment at 1400 hours on Friday, 19 January. By 1620 hours, we retracted from the beach, pulled up the ramp, and closed the bow doors. With the YMS-357 as escort, we were underway to Tinian Island in the Marianas. At 1000 hours the next morning, we were beached at Kammer Beach, Tinian Harbor to disembark the minemen and unload their equipment.

***

For the rest of the month of January, we made our rounds delivering equipment and supplies from Tinian to Saipan to Guam in repeated succession. The cargos included cane cars, lengths of rail, boxes of aircraft engines, and miscellaneous supplies. All of our deliveries were escorted by the YMS-357 which was equipped with one three inch .50 caliber dual purpose gun mount, two 20mm mounts, and two depth charge projectors. The minesweepers and sub chasers were always welcome company when we ventured into the open ocean.

***

Fighting was an inevitable occurrence when teenaged men were placed together in a cramped space for long periods of time. These fights tended to happen at night when senior officers or others in charge might not be around as much. Well, late one night very close to midnight, we were underway from Saipan to Tinian Island and I was on watch on the conn. The moon was near full and reflecting beautifully back at me from the waving Pacific. The peaceful interlude with my lunar companion was interrupted by a few loudly expressed profanities and the sound of fists meeting flesh. The disruption came from Gun #3 on the port side. I looked down just as the two gunners mates went at each other with a few more haymakers before it turned for the worse. One of the figures fell and popped right back up to lunge and spear the other guy in the midsection. This went on for a few more seconds before Ensign Merschel and another seaman arrived to break it up.

"You boys knock it off! Knock it off!"

Sailors were known for fighting over girls, insults to their heritage, or losing in a card or dice game. Boys would fight over someone stealing a cigarette from their pack, or a comment about a picture of a girlfriend taped to the wall in their rack. However, one of those fellows crossed the line with a comment he made about the other guy's girl.

"What is the meaning of this, men? You are both supposed to be on watch!"

"Well sir, he seems to not like the fact that my girlfriend is in an internment camp. He called me a 'dirty Jap lover'."

"Well. Is that so?" The ensign retorted with a raised eyebrow as he surveyed the boy with the Japanese girlfriend. Then, turning to the other fellow, he reproached,

"Who he has for a girlfriend is none of your business sailor! You'll have to answer to the captain in the morning. He'll decide at mast what to do about all this ruckus. Now get back to your posts!"

"Aye Sir!"

At 1000 hours sharp the next morning, Captain White found both men guilty of fighting on watch. Both men were sentenced to twenty hours extra duty. I'm not sure if the full moon was to blame, or just a couple of tired sailors. Maybe it was the rancid beans from the galley. We were always running on quick naps or just plain lack of sleep. Working the shifts that we were assigned didn't allow for getting sufficient rest.

***

On 9 February 1945, 1038 hours, we beached at the LST landing area of Talofofo Harbor, Guam to pick up Marine Engineers and their equipment. The LSM-143 took aboard a fully equipped Marine Engineering Battalion of the Third Marine Division consisting of fifty-five Marines and their necessary gear. The roster included two members from Headquarters and Service Company, three from B Company, and fifty from C Company. The equipment included one twelve and a half ton dump truck, one water trailer, one machinery trailer, one three eighths yards shovel, two TD18 bulldozers, one TD14 bulldozer, and two TD18 primer movers. At 1300 hours, all men were aboard, all equipment secure, and we were underway to Apra Harbor.

For the next six days, we made our rounds taking on fuel, fresh water, food stores, ammunition, and all other provisions we would need for the invasion of an island that we only knew as "*Island X*".

Assigned to Task Force 51.5, LSM Group Fourteen, Flotilla Five, LSM-143 left Guam at 1300 hours on 16 February destined to arrive at "*Island X*" on 20 February, D-Day plus one. Task Force 51.5 was possibly the largest armada of sea power ever assembled to this day. We fell into formation as the third of a column of six LSMs in company with countless LSTs, AKAs, APAs, destroyer escorts, submarine chasers, minesweepers, and the list went on and on.

One of the ships that we would be making the invasion with was the LST-477. On 12 February 1945, twenty-four Sherman tanks, five jeeps, one truck, two hundred ninety-eight enlisted men and sixteen officers of the 3rd Tank Battalion were loaded aboard LST-477 at Apra Harbor, Guam. On the sixteenth, the ship fell in line with several other LSTs including the LST-809 and the LST-646, both loaded down with tanks and Marines.

Also sailing in convoy with us on 16 February was the *AKN-4 (USS Keokuk).* The Keokuk was originally

commissioned in July of 1941 as a coastal minelayer (*CMc-6*) and later reclassified as a minelayer *(CM-8)*. It would be reclassified for the final time in November 1943 as a net cargo ship (*AKN-4*). A net cargo ship was fitted with two large aft doors that were designed for the laying of torpedo nets. As a minelayer, the doors served a similar purpose of strategic placing of mines.

Marines were assigned as gun watch for the 40mm and 20mm anti-aircraft guns aboard ship. Nothing was going to stop us on the way, or when we got to the island. The escorts, sub chasers, and minesweepers were going to get us there so that the rest of us could serve our packages to the enemy. We were a floating Hell on Earth, and we were ready to deliver it to the Japs.

***

We sounded general quarters; immediately all stations were manned and ready. For the first two hours, we commenced zig-zag pattern #6 with engines all ahead at two-thirds. By 1915 hours, we secured from zig-zag pattern #6 and fell into the convoy speed of two-thirds full.

Scuttlebutt had spread the word around the enlisted men the names of more than a hundred different islands that we were going to attack. After two days at sea, we learned from the sealed orders that came aboard exactly where we would be hitting the beach. The "scuttlebutt" always seemed to be way off the mark. One thing that we all realized, without the rumors from scuttlebutt, was that the Pacific was our battlefield. This was the moment. This was OUR moment. We were going to do our jobs, and move on to the next.

We discovered that we were zig-zagging our way to an island called Iwo Jima. At the time, it might as well have kept the name *"Island X"* because we had never heard of it and neither had anyone back home in the states. Within the next week, the whole world would know the name and what took place. Those who experienced it first-hand would never forget it, but prayed that they could. It would haunt their dreams, and fill survivors with the guilt of why they made it and their buddies didn't. Many of boys would take these nightmarish scenes to their graves. Some of the boys would just learn to cope with the nightmares.

The crew gathered around a map that displayed a small, ugly pork chop in the middle of the Pacific. Captain White pointed out the landing beaches that we were to transport the Marines and their equipment. The first would be a beach codenamed "*Green Beach*" that was the closest landing point possible to a hump on the map that he referred to as "*Mount Suribachi*". At the time, that name just went in one ear and entered into our minds as just another hill on a miserable little island with nothing but Japs and sand. Little did we know at the time, but that little "bump", and the island it was attached to on the map, would become a household name to the folks back home in just a matter of days. It should have been easy for us to find since the hill was the most noticeable landmark on the map. It also proved to be quite deadly.

The lead LSM had signaled a sighting of an enemy submarine to our starboard side. I pressed the general quarters button and immediately reached for the right handle and pulled downward to expose and hide the light through the flapping louvers in rhythmic patterns to reveal my "affirmative" reply back to the lead LSM. Ensign Juliana ordered us to make an emergency forty degree turn to port in an evasive move. A sub chaser got the signaled warning as well, and forged ahead at flank speed to meet the aggressor head on. The gunner on the sub chaser fired off a hedgehog round and waited. The hedgehog was designed to only explode on contact with a target. This would make sure that the explosion would not interfere with sonar making the sub chaser lose the target. He fired twice more with no detonation. We assumed that the enemy submarine fled because he disappeared from sonar and any visuals.

The next day, 18 February at 1221 hours, a mine was sighted by a destroyer escort and once again, we were placed under general quarters and had to make an evasive, emergency turn forty degrees to port around the mine. For the rest of the day and into the nineteenth, we were ordered to commence zig zag diagram #6 and a convoy speed of nine knots. Japanese submarines would emerge and then vanish from view the entire trip. We practically stayed in general quarters while we communicated constantly with the lead ship and our escorts. The escorts really had a tedious job. They were duteous about getting us through this maze of submarines and mines the Japanese had placed. We owe a debt of gratitude to those diligent men of the escorts.

***

At 2245 hours, 19 February, we received news from the radar room that we were within 40 miles of Iwo Jima. The men who had gone below decks came topside once they had gotten wind of the report. The first wave of Marines had hit the beach at 0859 earlier that morning, and we were bringing the next wave of Marines and equipment. We were steaming at two-thirds ahead through the menacing darkness. The water was an eerie calm except for the froth the screws churned out from the mass of ships. At 2258 hours, we witnessed the faintest flashes of light on the horizon off in the distance from the shelling the island was taking. The flashes from the direction of the island were like Morse code; at least that is how the rhythmic glinting struck me. I couldn't take my eyes off of the flashing light just above the horizon. It was like a forbidding sign of unavoidable dangers lying in wait to pounce on us like a hungry wolf. I closed my eyes and the flashing was burned in my memory with the message: Dah dit dit; dit; dit dah; dah; dit dit dit dit.

Chapter 9

THE HORNETS' NEST

Iwo Jima is a volcanic and sandy island that is five and a half miles long and two and a half miles at its widest point. The most recognizable physical feature of the island is a dormant volcano known as Mount Surabachi. At the time, the Navy had codenamed the ominous figure *"Hot Rocks"*. Mount Surabachi is the highest point of the island at one hundred sixty meters above sea level. Iwo To (Japanese name for the island) is translated as *"sulfur island"*, and the island is undeniably full of sulfur. This is evident by the yellow sulfuric mist that routinely rises from cracks of earth. The island very distinctly smells like rotten eggs. Iwo Jima is part of the Japanese Volcano Islands chain south of the Ogasawara Islands and together with them form the Ogasawara Archipelago also known as the Bonin Islands. The island of twenty-one square kilometers is six hundred fifty nautical miles south of mainland Tokyo and is administered as part of Ogasawara, one of the eight villages of Tokyo.

By the summer of 1943, the island had a civilian population of approximately 1,018 residing in six settlements. The island had one school, a Shinto shrine, and one police officer. It received its mail from the mainland once a month via mail ship and many of its consumer goods through trade. The economy of the inhabitants relied upon sulfur mining, sugarcane farming, and fishing. With the threat of an Allied invasion, the entire civilian population was evacuated in July of 1944, and never returned. With the removal of the civilians, it was uninhabited except for the twenty thousand Japanese soldiers burrowed in the complex tunnels underground. The tiny island was considered a strategic target mainly for the three air fields that it possessed. The United States felt that it would be an ideal place to deploy B-29s in bombing raids on the Japanese mainland.

In June 1944, Lieutenant General Tadamichi Kuribayashi was assigned to command the defense of Iwo Jima. Kuribayashi knew that Japan could not win the battle, but he hoped to inflict massive casualties on the American forces, so that the United States and its allies would reconsider carrying out the invasion of the Japanese mainland. The war of attrition that the Japanese were gambling on just inflated the American resolve and swelled our hatred. We were beyond just fighting an enemy and liberating the Pacific islands and their inhabitants. We abhorred the Japanese. The Japanese loathed Americans. That's what made it WAR. We had heard horror stories of Marines tied to trees on Guadalcanal with body parts severed and lying around the body. The Japanese had used our boys for bayonet practice. Military men tend to not kill people they just "dislike". If that were so, we could just play a quick game of badminton, and the winner gets the Pacific. The phrase *"war is hell"* was derived from an 1880 speech by William Tecumseh Sherman. The Civil War Union General went on the say, *"I am sick and tired of war. Its glory is all moonshine. It is only those who have neither fired a shot nor heard the shrieks and groans of the wounded who cry aloud for blood, for vengeance, for desolation. War is hell."*

While drawing inspiration from the defense of Peleliu, Kuribayashi designed a defense that broke with Japanese military doctrine. Rather than establishing his defenses on the beach to face the landings directly, he created strong, mutually supporting defenses in depth using static, heavy weapons such as heavy machine guns and artillery. Takeichi Nishi's armored tanks were to be used as camouflaged artillery positions. Because the tunnel linking the mountain to the main forces was never completed, Kuribayashi organized the southern area of the island in and around Mount Suribachi as a semi-independent sector, with his main defensive zone built up in the north. The expected American naval and air bombardment further prompted the creation of an extensive system of tunnels that connected the prepared positions, so that a pillbox that had been cleared could be reoccupied. This network of bunkers and pillboxes favored the Japanese defenses. Hundreds of hidden artillery and mortar positions along with land mines were placed all over the island. Among the Japanese weapons were 320mm spigot mortars and a variety of explosive rockets.

Numerous Japanese snipers and camouflaged machine gun positions were also set up. Kuribayashi specially engineered the defenses so that every part of Iwo Jima was subject to Japanese defensive fire. He also received a handful of kamikaze pilots to use against the enemy fleet. Three hundred eighteen American sailors were killed by kamikaze attacks during the battle. However, against his wishes, Kuribayashi's superiors on Honshu ordered him to erect some beach defenses. These were the only parts of his defenses that were destroyed during the pre-landing bombardment.

Starting on 15 June 1944, the U.S. Navy and the U.S. Army Air Forces began naval bombardments and air raids against Iwo Jima, which would become the longest and most intense in the Pacific theater. They contained a combination of naval artillery shellings and aerial bombings that went on for nine months. Major General Harry Schmidt of the Marine Corps requested a 10-day heavy shelling of Iwo Jima before the amphibious assault, but was given only three days, and these were impaired by the weather conditions. Each heavy warship was given an area on which to fire that, combined with all the ships, covered the entire island. Each warship fired for approximately six hours before stopping for a predetermined length of time.

The American bombings and bombardments continued through 19 February 1945, D-Day for the amphibious landing. The invasion would be codenamed *Operation Detachment* with a scheduled H-hour of 0900 hours. The limited bombardment had questionable success on the enemy due to the Japanese being heavily dug-in and fortified. However, many bunkers and caves were destroyed during the bombing giving it some limited success. The Japanese had been preparing for this battle since March 1944, which gave them a significant head start. By the time of the landing, about four hundred fifty American ships were located off Iwo Jima. The entire battle involved about sixty thousand U.S. Marines and several thousand U.S. Navy Seabees.

At 0859 hours, one minute ahead of schedule, the first of an eventual thirty thousand Marines of the 3rd, 4th, and 5th Marine Divisions, making up the V Amphibious Corps, landed on the beach. The initial wave did not come under Japanese fire for some time, as General Kuribayashi's plan was to wait until the beach was full of the Marines and their equipment. Then, he would unleash his rain of Hell on them.

When the word reached the general that the American fleet was underway, he delivered an impassioned speech to his men. He employed them with the following words:

"Men. The time has come to show your true colors. As a member of the honorable Imperial Army, I trust that you will fight with honor. This island is of utmost importance to Japan. Should the island fall, the enemy will use it as their base to attack our homeland. For our homeland, fight until the very last man. Our duty is to stop the enemy right here. Not one of

you is allowed to die until you have killed ten enemy soldiers. Do not expect to return home alive. I will always be in front of you."

Then, Kuribayashi removed his hat and led his men in a feverish round of *"Bonsai!"* as they raised both arms to the sky. As the last voice echoed through the tunnels, the room fell silent. General Kuribayashi placed his hat back on his head and proudly strolled to his post.

***

19 January 1945 was our 'D-Day' and 0900 was H-hour for the invasion of Iwo Jima, but our convoy wasn't scheduled to arrive until the morning of 20 February. By 0900 hours on the twentieth, the island was in plain view. Of course, we had trained for landings on the California beaches, and San Clemente Island. We had trained landing Marines, tanks, and so forth. Our whole training had built up to that one battle at Iwo Jima. We had Marine engineers and their equipment on board. The mission of the LSTs and LSMs was not to transport troops on D-Day, but to deliver the engineers, their equipment, and tanks once the first wave of Marines established a beachhead. The LSM-143 was one of thirty-one LSMs that would participate in operations at Iwo Jima. We were in a convoy of ships steaming to make our deliveries. Our column leader, AKN-4 (USS Keokuk), was positioned to our port bow. We were steaming just astern the LST-809 with the LST-477 abeam to our starboard. The LST-790 was situated just to

starboard of the LST-809; dead ahead of the LST-477. Those were the same ships we were among when we left Guam just four days prior. As I scanned the horizon, there were ships as far as I could see in every direction. Bad weather and strong winds produced a four-foot surf that disrupted our landings. The high surf and the strong undertow made maintaining a landing challenging for the LSTs and LSMs. So, many of the landings were postponed until the weather improved.

The following day, LST-477 developed steering trouble and dropped astern until control could be regained. The entire convoy had scaled our speed back to one third in order to stay in formation to allow the ship to fix the problem. Zig zag diagram #6 was also maintained to elude Japanese submarine attacks. We were ordered to commence and cease the zig zag diagram every half hour to an hour in order to confuse the enemy.

The morning of 21 February at 0825 hours aboard the LST-477, a young communications officer, Lieutenant Vinson Reinhard was demonstrating to David Bartol (Signalman First Class) how to disable the "*IFF*" (*Identification Friend or Foe*) transmitter on the ship's radar. The detonator, which he held in his hand, exploded, critically wounding him. Bartol was thrown to the ground by the blast, but received only minor injuries. In case of an abandon ship, it was the communication officer's duty to destroy the radar and the log books. We didn't want our radars to get into the Japs hands by any means.

We didn't want our ships logs to be taken by the enemy either. So there are explosive charges on the radars. Something went wrong this time, and the thing exploded and killed him. Despite everything the ship's corpsman R.E. Fletcher could muster, Lieutenant Vinson Reinhard died soon afterwards. Lieutenant Reinhard's injuries were described in the casualty report as a traumatic hemorrhage, severance of the right carotid artery, contributory wounds, and severe shock. David Bartol, S1c, was taken to his rack located in the forward starboard side to recover from his wounds.

We did something that you just don't do in war time. The whole convoy came to a stop, and we had a burial at sea for this young officer. Captain James G. Sampson officiated the ceremony with the reading of passages from the Bible followed by prayer. The U.S. Ensign on the LST-477 was ordered flown at half-mast at 1402 hours. At latitude 24 degrees 13' North and 141 degrees 56' East, Lieutenant Reinhard was committed to the sea with volleys from a 3rd Marines Tank Battalion firing squad. It was actually a beautiful thing when all the sailors and Marines lined up along the deck in salute as the honored sailor slid into the deep. There's not a greater honor in the world than the reverence placed on a military funeral. However, to stop a convoy in a warzone was dangerous business; we never knew if a submarine was shadowing or chasing us. Immediately following the ceremony, our convoy carried on.

***

Kamikazes! We didn't know this navy fodder as anything but *"Kamikazes"*. *Kamikaze* is translated as *"divine wind"* which was the name usually reserved for the suicide units attacking from the sky. This strategy combining all of the different suicide methods was called *"Tokko"* or *"Tokko Tai"* abbreviated from the official term *"Tokubetsu Kogekitai"* which literally translates as *"special attack unit"*. Kamikazes were all volunteer fighters that would crash into a ship to put it out of commission. Many historians would argue that instead of being patriots, who willingly sacrificed themselves for Japan, kamikazes were actually vulnerable young men who were radicalized or pressured by fanatics into pursuing an "honorable" death. Many times they just flew fighter planes,

187

dive bombers, or whatever would fly filled with explosives in the hull, or they carried bombs and torpedoes. The pilots all had last rites before take-off because they knew they would crash their airplane into a ship and blow up. They figured it was all a suicide mission. It was quite a common thing for a long time. I don't think we were the first bunch of ships that had ever been under attack by Kamikazes and definitely not the last. *"Kamikaze"* was a known name, a factor that we had to take into consideration. There *WOULD* be Kamikazes! We were under pressure every minute. They very seldom sank a ship, but they could undeniably put a ship out of commission.

The beliefs of these Japanese date all the way back to the fourteenth century Samurai. The Samurai developed the military code of the Bushido. One of the rules of Bushido is that in the event of disgrace or defeat, the warrior MUST commit suicide. Ceremonial suicide was not to be judged as a weakness, but as an act of the greatest moral strength. The code of the fourteenth century Samurai was a convenient concept for the modern Japanese military leaders to adopt. The Japanese reached into their medieval past and tied an old concept meshed with the modern weapons. The volunteer pilots were asked to commit controlled suicide. The idea was explained to the young airmen that if they dived into the enemy ships, the weak American spirit would be broken.

The Kamikaze was a terrifying weapon that was conceived by the Japanese in desperation. The "volunteer" pilots committed themselves to an unthinkable violent end as a human bomb. The young men's engrained loyalty to an emperor "god", would willingly hurtle themselves into oblivion. The idea was first introduced after the Japanese loss at Guadalcanal in February of 1943. The concept was originally rejected by some Japanese strategists as "defeatist" and was considered out of the question. Then, with the realization that the Americans could not be defeated by conventional means, the idea was eventually accepted. The goal was to inflict overwhelming casualties on the Americans to destroy their will to fight. They rationalized the idea that a single man in a single plane traded for the destruction of an American aircraft carrier justified the horrific means.

The leaders of the German Luftwaffe had proposed a similar tactic as a result of the relentless Allied bombing on German cities. Overwhelming hatred toward the Americans after the bombings killed thousands of civilian men, women, and children fueled the volunteers into action. The Luftwaffe group, *Sonderkommando Elbe,* was assigned to ram unsuspecting B-24 Liberators and B-17 Flying Fortresses on their way to missions on key German targets. Barely one month before the mission, three hundred German pilots volunteered with the understanding that there was only a ten percent chance of survival. The mission was not intended to be suicidal. Each pilot was instructed to eject either on or just moments before impact in order to return to base to prepare for subsequent attacks. The Germans had managed to organize only one such mission on April 7, 1945 employing stripped down versions of the Messerschmitt Me-109. The armor intended to protect the pilot was taken off to allow more maneuverability and faster attack dives. The aircraft for the mission were armed with only sixty rounds of ammunition in a lone machine gun, the MG-131. The pilots were quickly trained to ram one of three vulnerable areas on the bombers in hopes of stopping or delaying the Allied bombing. The mission yielded dismal results and failed in any attempt to stop the Allied onslaught against the "vaterland".

Vice Admiral of the Imperial Japanese Navy Takijiro Onishi was tasked with organizing the Japanese attack units. At first, like many other Japanese leaders, Onishi opposed the idea and stated that it was "heresy". But with losses at the Philippines and the Marianas, he felt it was the only choice. He enlisted volunteers from the 201st Naval Air Group in the Philippines and had no time for specialized training. Many of the first volunteers were dive bomber pilots with experience in performing near vertical dives. The initial success gave the Japanese confidence that this tactic could turn the tides in their favor. As the war progressed, the number of experienced pilots quickly dwindled. The Imperial Japanese Navy (*IJN*) began enlisting inexperienced pilots using any flyable aircraft available to continue the onslaught. Most of these boys were no more than trainees. They were generally given two days of take-off training, two days of formation flying, and three days of actually how to dive into an enemy ship. They trained for about a week, and were asked to use themselves as a human-guided torpedo.

One day after the announcement was made that the Japanese forces had surrendered; Onishi committed ritual suicide on 16 August 1945. He wrote a suicide note apologizing to the almost four thousand pilots whom he had sent to their deaths, and offered his death as reparation to the pilots and their families.

Although there had been impromptu suicide strikes from wounded Japanese planes with no other choice, the first organized Kamikaze mission occurred at Leyte Gulf on 25 October 1944. The Zeroes in this mission were fitted with a five hundred pound bomb in place of the external fuel tank. The extra weight rendered the A6M unable to engage in a dogfight if they encountered American opposition. The planners of the mission sent along four additional Zeroes as escorts to keep any American planes at bay. The USS Saint Lo (*former USS Midway*) was the first American ship to be sunk by a Kamikaze. When the plane struck the American carrier, it set off a domino of explosions from fuel tanks, munition magazines, and aircraft. It was viewed as such a colossal success, that the attacks would be repeated almost three thousand more times. This one attack justified the vision that the Japanese could take one plane and destroy an entire ship and kill hundreds of men. These attacks would claim five thousand American lives and wound four thousand eight hundred more before the war's end. Ominously, Japan reserved approximately five thousand Kamikaze aircraft for the expected American invasion of the home islands. The devastation quite possibly could have been doubled.

Katori Naval Air Base near Yokosuka, Honshu, was established in February 1944 with two runways designed into a crisscross pattern. In February 1945, the Kamikaze Special Attack Corps 2nd Mitate ("*Imperial shield*") Unit was formed from the 601st Air Group. The squadron included twelve *Yokosuka D4Y Suisei* two-seat carrier dive bombers (nicknamed "*Judy*" by the Allies), eight *Nakajima B6N Tenzan* (nicknamed "*Jill*") three-seat carrier attack bombers, and twelve escorting *Mitsubishi A6M Zero* fighters. The 2nd Mitate Unit led by Lieutenant Hiroshi Murakawa took off from Katori on 20 February 1945 enroute to Iwo Jima but were forced to return to base due to poor weather.

In the early morning of 21 February 1945, the 2nd Mitate Unit took off again from Katori Air Base. After the aircraft refueled at Hachijojima Island about one hundred twenty-five miles south of Tokyo Bay, the Japanese squadron set their course for the American fleet near Iwo Jima. They were on a collision course scheduled to assault the US Navy later that evening.

The planes flew at wave-top level to avoid radar detection by the American fleet. Stealth was of the essence in order to insure maximum success of the mission. The A6M Zeroes were along on the mission to provide fighter escort to ensure the suicide planes got to their targets, and to report back on any results of the attacks. The escorts were not to engage the enemy unless absolutely necessary, and were to report back to base as soon as possible with the details.

The two best approaches to attack a ship were either extremely high or extremely low angles depending on the situation. During the high angle attack, the Kamikaze approached from twenty thousand feet at twenty degrees. Then, when the aircraft reached five thousand feet, it changed into a steep, high-speed, fifty degree dive to the target. For the low angle attack, the plane approached at below forty feet above the water to avoid radar detection. When he neared the target, the pilot pulled up to fifteen hundred feet and began the dive. This technique relied on speed and gravity to reach the ship, even if the plane was hit by flak. Since there were so many American radar screens probing the skies, the low angle technique was used most in the waters off Iwo Jima.

***

By 1710 hours, we had motored on during the past three hours leisurely circling in uneventful bliss in our night retirement area. The ships in the retirement area were constantly underway unless they were tied up to an APA or AKA to take on cargo or troops. This gave the enemy a more difficult target to attack from above or below.

The weather was sullen with an overcast sky and an icy breeze that would just cut right through. I pulled together my jacket collar and secured the top button. Raising my shoulders, I cupped my hands, took a breath, and blew. I could see the smoke from my breath hitting the cold air as it escaped my fingers. I hurriedly rubbed my hands together hoping the friction would warm my palms. It helps some, but I just resolved to put my hands in my pockets until it was time to do my job.

Every ship had a small signal light on the yardarm to communicate with the ships in all directions. Otherwise, the large, louvered light was used to communicate to a particular ship especially during the daylight hours. The light provided us with some warmth if you could stay close to it. Our ship had two signalmen, George Cimbala and me, with shifts of four hours of bridge duty. The signal light was equipped with a louvered flapper with a handle on both sides that allowed the signaler to flash the code to approaching planes or ships. I kept in close contact that day with the ship dead ahead of me. There we were with engines at one third steaming toward the beach. We were about a half day out to sea on our way to Iwo Jima. The battleships and the heavy cruisers laid off the shore probably about half mile out in the ocean shelling "Hot

Rocks". You could hear them day and night, just shhhooo…shhhoooo…shhhooo. Those big projectiles could be heard going overhead.

The entire Navy had supper at the same time. At suppertime, our own planes flew cover over us. They were generally Marine F4U Corsairs that circled over the convoy as we were approaching Iwo Jima. Come supper time, they said *"Well, the heck with this, we're going to supper"*. They went back to their carrier, landed, and headed to mess for supper. The sky was conspicuous with all this lack of aircraft. I remember Ensign Bryan saying, *"Garforth, why are there no planes overhead?"*

I just looked up, surveyed the sky, and replied, *"They are always gone about this time of day sir. I guess they are having their supper."*

"Alright Garforth. Keep your eyes peeled for Nips. I don't want any surprises."

"Aye sir."

I wasn't exactly sure that was the case, but we noticed that the whistling sound from the engine air inlets on the inverted gull wings were absent from the symphony of sounds which we were exposed to on a daily basis. This distinctive sound gave way to the Japanese nickname for the F4U Corsair as *"Whistling Death"*. The nickname was well deserved. The Marines in those Corsairs flew fearlessly against the Japanese airmen and while delivering napalm to the shore. I would see them get as close to the target as humanly possible, then pull out at the last minute when they delivered their ordinances. It was awe-inspiring.

While our air cover was gone, the Japanese were aware of this, so they would come around when there was no one there to protect us. The Japanese were good at timing their strikes; hitting their enemy when they were the most vulnerable.

The radar on every ship was manned 100%. Harvey Hobert (*Radarman Third Class - RdM3c*), saw what he thought was our planes because they gave a signal that they were "friendly" which shows up on the radar. He saw lots of aircraft on the radar and just assumed it was our cover. That was the report we received, but it was wrong. By the time we realized it was the enemy, it was too late.

At 1718 hours, I just so happened to train my eyes up at the ominous gray clouds when five aircraft emerged from the center like hornets from a nest. With their engines wound tight and whining, one banked to the right then made a low left bank. I got just the slightest glance of the olive green beast with fiery red circles on the bottom of each wing. As soon as I saw the plane, I pressed the general quarters button, and the horns began to wail. It was a *Yokosuka D4A* dive bomber referred to by the Allies as a *"Judy"* with landing gears extended in the down position. The *Judy* had a crew of two including the pilot and a gunner and was carrying two 250 kilogram bombs. I looked back astern to our starboard side at the plane as it skimmed along about forty feet above the water coming right toward our convoy. I was looking straight at the nose of this plane almost grazing the water. The plane set its sights on the starboard side of the LST-477. Just before impact, the pilot began strafing with the 7.7mm forward machine guns producing the pinging of metal to metal. It sounded like the times we would throw hands full of gravels at a piece of tin roofing when we were kids. The Japanese dive bomber rammed the ship just forward to where signalman David Bartol was recovering from his wounds sustained during the radar explosion just three hours previous. The young signalman was blown from his rack and killed instantly along with several of his comrades.

The LST-477 had been limping behind ever since its

steering went out; they were the slowest target on which the Japanese pilots locked. A monstrous explosion from the two bombs on the aircraft sent the elevator, deck debris, and smoke up a hundred feet into the air. The concussion from the blast was deafening. A gigantic cloud of orange fire and black smoke flared from the ship. The five-ton elevator made some cartwheels before slamming itself edgewise into the opening from which it was dislodged. The LST's 40mm and 20mm opened fire topside as the Marines helped with the guns, working as loaders, fighting fires, and throwing hot ready ammunition overboard. From my post on our conning tower, I was in awe of the devastation. I couldn't believe my eyes. I had heard about these attacks, but I never believed it would happen to our convoy.

The second assailant to strike just moments after the LST-477 was an enemy "*Jill*" (*Nakajima B6N Tenzan*). The gun crew of the LST-809 had gotten to its guns and opened fire on the enemy plane striking a severe blow that left it flaming and smoking as it hit the *USS Keokuk (AKN-4)* on its starboard side. The plane struck the flying bridge and continued to the starboard deck, where a bomb exploded abreast of the sick bay, blowing a hole in the deck and completely wrecking the sick bay. Fires were alive on the flying bridge, starboard motor whale boat, sick bay, laundry room, radio room, motor generator room, and .50 caliber magazine. A gasoline fire erupted on deck from the area above sick bay back to the aft wenches on the starboard side of the ship.

The explosion was deafening with flying metal and smoke filling the evening air. The devastation knocked out the starboard 20mm battery on the Keokuk, and left a gaping hole in the side. The smell of burning grease and oil filled the air as it wafted by my post.

I heard more flak from the LST-809, and when I looked to port, the gunner had hit another plane that was smoking and bearing down on my position. I looked down from the bridge, and the "Judy" was just forward of the bridge. The big, red meatball insignia on the top of the wings was the second I had seen that day and the closest that I ever wanted to get to a Jap plane. From my vantage point, I could see the determined face of the pilot concentrating straight ahead trying to hit his mark. I ducked behind the walls of the conn for what little protection that I thought I could gain. The plane flashed over our loaded well deck between the conning tower and the 40mm gun mount on the bow. If he had hit, the whole ship would have gone up in flames. It was on a flight patterned aimed right at me. I raised back up as he passed and I could see that he barely passed over the ships rail. If it had come two feet shorter it would have hit the side of the ship, which is what he was trying to do! Thankfully, he was a little bit high, or we were a little bit small. He just barely missed us! He went right over the front of our ship to the point that I could look down on him. His plane went out of control, wobbling down and left as he struck the water about fifty yards beyond us. Fire and metal blew in all directions. Geysers of water sprayed skyward. The pilot was a piece of raw hamburger in a flight suit that hit the side of our ship just forward of the conn. It was enough to make anyone sick. I mean, when he hit the water, the explosion blew his airplane apart, and it propelled him about fifty yards into the side of our ship. His lifeless body just went SPLAT into the side of the ship and went to the bottom. Out in the distance, I watched what was left of his airplane rise and fall with the wake. Then, in just seconds, it slowly sank below the waves.

I've never been so scared in my life. My knees were knocking, and I kept talking to myself. I said, "*Quiet down Garforth, if he's gonna hitcha, he's gonna hitcha. Nothin' you can do about it*". There was no means to help the stricken ships. A ship was absolutely on its own during an invasion. We had our orders to keep going, thankful he missed us, and concerned for the LST-477 to our beam that took a hit. We were concerned for everyone that got hit. We realized that if he had been strafing when he was running on us, it would have been our end; the Marines had trucks on board loaded with flame-thrower fuel. The whole ship would have gone up like a rocket, and we all would have lost our lives.

Two other Kamikazes flew passed the 143, and into a hospital ship. I just glanced over to see the explosion on the hospital. Hospitals were well marked with all white and a huge red cross painted on the sides and the top. It was an agreement between the combatants that hospital ships were not attacked, so duty there was usually relatively safe. It should have been; it was taking care of the wounded that were being brought aboard. Hospital ships should not be concerned about being bombed or attacked by an aircraft. However, that's the kind of opponents the Japanese were at the time. The Japanese pre-invasion briefings on the island contained a line item to target the corpsmen wearing the distinctive white band with a red cross. Their logic implied that if the Americans aren't able to help their wounded, more will die. I wondered if the Japanese Air Forces had the same such meeting with their pilots. Two of them struck a hospital ship, killing scores on board.

Everything was going on all around us. Total chaos was everywhere. In that kind of situation, a guy needed eyes in the back of his head. They came all at once at our convoy. We had one twin 40mm gun, five 20mm, and two 50-caliber guns. We had enough to make quite a hole in something. Unfortunately, our guns never got a chance to fire, and our guns were our only defense. We had to shoot them down before they can get to our ship. Although our guns were manned, the attack was so sudden and the ceiling so low, that we didn't get the guns into operation until the plane had passed, and then it was impossible to fire without endangering the rest of the convoy. I think that was why their initial approach of attack was so low; they knew that we wouldn't chance hitting our own ships with friendly fire.

I always wondered if that boy on the LST-477 would have survived the attack if he had been at his signalman's post on the conning tower that day. Just when we thought a job was relatively safe, the enemy found a way to make us think again. No job was safe when the Japanese were involved. There wasn't a man in the entire fleet that had that luxury. The Japs weren't just ON that smoldering island, they were UNDER the island, IN the air, and UNDER the water. They were EVERYWHERE!

I remember as a boy walking in the woods and stumbling into a small hole. All of the sudden I felt intense stinging on my legs. When I looked down, scores of yellow jackets were on and inside my trousers delivering their painful venom into my legs. I bolted and ran, and before I could beat them out of my pant legs, I had been stung a dozen times. That was the kind of enemy we were fighting. They were under every crack and crevice on the island. They were under every wave in the water. They were behind every cloud in the air. There wasn't a man with idle time from the signalmen, to the radarmen, to the radiomen, and the gunners. Name any rating and they were on their toes with eyes in the back of their heads.

***

When the melee subsided, crewmen aboard the LST-477 used emergency fire pumps, drawing water from lines thrown over the side. The ensuing action was described by a ship's officer, Lt. Cowden: "*It was mechanical trouble with the steering gear that got us into the wrong spot. In the surprise attack the Japs went gunning for the tail-end ship, which was us. There was no warning of enemy action, although all ships were standing routine gun watch. It was amazing how they came in so close without being detected. A lookout reported planes in the clouds, and almost before he finished the words they were coming out of the overcast sky 800 yards away.*"

The gun crews remained at their stations despite the fires and exploding ammunition with shell fragments flying around. Power was out on the LST due to the blast and the fire was nearing the forward magazine. The fire hoses were temporarily useless; only a few emergency pumps worked. LST-477 was dead in the water with the convoy moving ahead. Throughout the air attack and fire that followed, the Marines of the 3rd Tank Battalion fought side by side with the ship's company, manning guns and fire hoses, heaving hot ammunition over the side, and helping care for the wounded. There actually was a Japanese pilot who jumped out in a parachute when his plane was shot down. Watching the parachute astern on the starboard side slowly drop into the water some crewmen standing next to a Marine remarked that *"I bet if we gave a rifle to one of these Marines he would shoot the devil before he hits the water."* A ship's officer issued orders that there would be no firing upon the Japanese pilot in the water. No attempt was seen to pick him up.

Five aircraft had attacked the convoy and no aircraft survived. With LST-477 dead in the water with no (electric) power, Blaine Heinze, Motor Machinist Mate Second Class,

fought his way through the fire over hot ammunition to the fourth deck emergency pump room. In the darkness and partially flooded space he succeeded in starting the pump and remained with it until pressure was restored in the fire mains. With all this, to one Marine looking for the rest of the convoy, the ships seemed to him to be miles ahead, ready to disappear in the distance. All of a sudden it got very lonely. Many waist type life belts had been inflated by the small pressurized bottle and could be heard going "pooch." The ship's Commanding Officer, Charles T. Hazelrigg, U.S.N.R., was determined to beach and unload the cargo. Debris littered the shapnel riddled tank deck, the five ton elevator was hanging sidewise into the opening so that it blocked the tank deck ramp. Two compartments forward were punctured through the bottom and water jetted in faster than the pumps could remove it, adding weight to the ship's bow down far below proper draft for beaching. Cargo was shifted aft as fuel and water tanks were filled to the limit. Men entered the bottom tanks forward and actually bailed out water to get the last gallons.

A search for the dead and survivors was led by the ship's corpsman, R. E. Fletcher. Many of the men he had the gruesome task of identifying were badly burned and some had to be identified by their dental records. The ship's captain, Lieutenant J.C. Cowden, entered the casualty list into the LST-477 deck log. The remains of the Japanese fliers were found in the well deck thrown from their aircraft and horribly burned. The sailors identified by "Doc" Fletcher were R.V. Jones, S2c; C.E. Minton, S1c; D.A. Bartol, SM1c; H.E. Hedrick, S1c; M.O. Seiler, F2c; J.C. Rainier, S1c. The Marines were identified as C.R. Axenroth, Corporal; J.H. McAdow, Corporal; and Kris Kristensen, Jr, Pfc.

For the second time in as many days, the LST-477 conducted a burial at sea. On 22 February 1945 at 1430 hours, personnel killed in action aboard the LST-477 were buried in position 24 degrees 41' N and 141 degrees 19' E. The scene was an eerie replay of the day before with the sailors and

Marines on board lined up at attention. Once again a volley was fired by the 3rd Marine Tank Battalion as the six sailors and three Marines killed in the Kamikaze attack were committed to the sea. This time, Reverand William H Turner (Lieutenant USNR) officiated the ceremony aboard the ship.

The five wounded, of which three were stretcher cases, were removed to the USS PA-206. Just as the last man was being loaded to the small boat, an air raid alarm was sounded holding the small boat with the wounded alongside. Enemy planes had been spotted on the horizon, but had changed direction away from the LST-477. A sigh of relief was felt around the wounded ship that had suffered miserably the last two days. Once the LST was cleared from general quarters, the PA-206 was released to the hospital ship.

With grim determination and untiring work from a ship repair party, the LST-477 limped its way to shore. On 24 February at 1328 hours, tanks rolled off LST-477 onto Green Beach I of Iwo Jima. By 1413 hours all tanks and personnel of the 3rd Tank Battalion were ashore and the proud ship pulled anchor and backed out full throttle into the open sea.

***

Meanwhile, aboard the Keokuk, the crew feverishly fought the flames for over an hour. The fires were finally extinguished by 1850 hours. Lieutenant Roger S Strout, officer on deck, entered the information concerning the damage from the attack and the casualty report. After a survey of the devastation, the corpsman found that the crew had suffered seventeen killed and forty-four wounded in the action. As a result of the bomb explosion of the fire following, the starboard motor whale boat, Captain's gig, and numbers five, seven, and nine life rafts were lost with all equipment.

After laboring for most the night trying to identify and tag the dead and wounded, the Keokuk maneuvered alongside the USS Hocking (APA-121) to transfer the forty-four wounded sailors for further medical treatment. At 1100 hours, a burial at sea ceremony was conducted for the seventeen men killed in action.

The Keokuk received "patched" repairs while at Iwo Jima and the crew continued to do their duty by delivering water to several ships in the fleet for several days after the attack. The ship was ordered to go to Leyte for more substantial repairs before getting underway to Okinawa on 19 March. The ship's mission was to arrive at Kerama Retto on 26 March to lay antisubmarine nets in preparation for the coming invasion of Okinawa. With D-Day (*1 April*) at hand, the AKN-4 continued to lay the submarine nets until it was ordered to depart for Saipan on 4 April. Before the war was over, the Keokuk (AKN-4) would receive five battle stars for her service in World War II.

***

Fifty kamikaze pilots from the 22d Mitate Special Attack Unit left Katori Airbase near Yokosuka and flung themselves against the ships on the outer perimeter of Iwo Jima that day. They had staged a plan for a strategic three hour attack on as many ships as possible. Thirty miles from where we were attacked, the kamikazes sank the escort carrier Bismarck Sea with heavy loss of life. They damaged several other ships, including the veteran Saratoga, finally knocked out of the war. The Lunga Point (CVE) was also damaged but was later repaired to full strength. By the end of the Battle of Iwo Jima, a total of three hundred fifty-eight Marines and sailors had been killed as a result of the kamikaze attacks.

***

When the smoke cleared, we set a course to rejoin the convoy and carry on with our mission. I looked back at the LST-477 and the USS Keokuk with a heavy heart. The ships were smoldering and they both were complete infernos. I had a helpless feeling that they were going to sink and everyone on board was going to die. The elevator of the LST-477 had knifed itself back into the well deck, and I could hear the frantic voices of the men fighting the fires and looking for their buddies. At the time, I didn't know who was hurt or how many. I felt like we were abandoning them, but we had a duty to perform. All sailors understood that when there was a mission, it couldn't be stopped for anything.

When George Cimbala relieved me that night at 1800 hours for his shift, I couldn't force myself to go below to my rack. I stayed topside and stared out into the sea at all the ships.

Maybe I thought my fate would be the same as the signalman on the 477. Maybe I was just too keyed up to rest. Whatever the reason, I just stood there alone with my thoughts. By that time, the LST-477 and the USS Keokuk were out of sight, but they were not out of mind. I kept playing the scene in my mind over and over again. I kept thinking, *"What if that plane had struck us amidships? Sixty-five men could have been killed or wounded, including me."* Where I was standing, I would have been the first to go.

It would be several days later that we got word that the ships had extinguished the fires and were both underway again. I couldn't believe that the LST-477 had even landed its cargo just days after the attack, and the Keokuk had laid nets around Okinawa just a month later. My hat's off to that brave crew of sailors on the Keokuk and the LST-477. Furthermore, I was always proud to be part of the "sandscraping" fraternity that was the LSTs and LSMs. They took a beating, got knocked down, but they NEVER stayed down.

Chapter 10

THE UNRELENTING MENACE

Operation Detachment (D-Day+2):   Wednesday, 21 February at 1830 hours, found us in the convoy just to port of the LST-943, and still under *Condition I Mike* making various courses and speeds to keep up. The kamikaze attack from just an hour before kept us on high alert. By 1907 hours, I was ordered to *"Flash White"* to the lead ship and we were secured from general quarters and set to *Condition II*. Condition I Mike is a US Naval condition which was essentially our *"general quarters"*. Its meaning to the crew is instinctive; indicating that an attack was present or imminent and the ship is at its highest state of alert. *Condition II* indicates that a threat is probable, but not present and the crew's readiness is somewhat more relaxed than full readiness. *Condition II* was usually ordered directly following *Condition I*. For practice sake, Ensign Merschel ordered me to *"Flash Red"* and sound general quarters to keep the men on their toes in case of another attack. From 1900 hours up until 2000 hours, we had sounded and secured general quarters three times. His thinking was to make sure that we weren't caught off guard again in case the Japs made another run on us.

General Quarters!

We slept in our clothes unless we were way out of the war zone. We didn't sleep in pajamas or shorts because we never knew when we had to come bailing out of there and get to our stations. Every man on that ship had a helmet, and we knew where it was at every second of the time. When I went on watch on the bridge, I took my helmet with me. I wore it! We never knew when someone was going to shoot at us.

The evening following the Kamikaze attacks found us in the night retirement area making circles and biding our time once again to allow the weather to improve for landing the Marine Engineers. The Navy had alerts that carry two parts to cut down on friendly fire and gave us better odds of firing upon the enemy. *"Flash Red"* meant that enemy aircraft had been identified in the area and air attack was imminent. Other possible codes were *"Flash Blue"* indicating that unidentified aircraft had been detected, and *"Flash White"* indicating the sky was clear of enemy or unidentified aircraft. Adding *"Control Green"* meant that there were friendly aircraft in the vicinity and fire could only be opened upon positive identification of the target as "enemy". The other option was *"Control Yellow"* which meant there were no friendlies nearby and anything in the air was fair game.

The Unrelenting Menace

Operation Detachment (D-Day+3): At 1400 hours, 22 February, we were underway making our circles in the retirement area. There was something going on all the time.

The Japs were attacking. The Marines in their Corsairs weren't flying cover every minute. Every afternoon, the Japs would come and bomb or strafe everything that was moving. We were under attack just anytime. We never knew when an enemy plane was coming over. We were always in a night retirement area because we just didn't operate at night. Well, we just couldn't see well enough at night to make landings. We were out at sea and we didn't have any street lights. So, we would be out in the deep water, probably a mile or two out at sea just making circles, slow circles just biding our time.

At 1530 hours, our radarman, Harvey Hobert, alerted our

crew of five enemy aircraft *"bearing 345 degrees relative,*

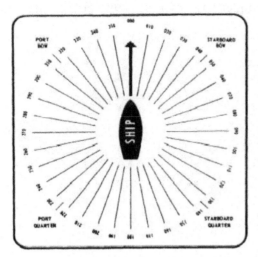

altitude low". The general quarters whistle wailed and the announcement over the intercom followed:

"Now hear this. General quarters. General quarters. All hands to battle stations. Enemy aircraft approaching. Bearing three-four-five. Range ten miles and closing fast."

Roughly translating the radar information, the Jap planes were spotted heading almost directly toward us off our port bow. "Relative bearing" used the direction that the bow is pointing as zero degrees. In a clockwise direction, this went all the way around the ship until three hundred sixty degrees reached the bow again. *"Three hundred forty-five degrees relative"* would have placed them directly in the path of our 40mm twin on the bow which was manned by the pointer Verlin Smith and his crew. That was not good news for the Japs heading toward us. We were immediately placed under *"Flash Red-Control Yellow"* which indicated that we there were enemy aircraft in the area (*Flash Red*), and no friendly aircraft (*Control Yellow*). This meant we could fire at will without the concern for accidentally striking our own planes.

When I heard "*altitude low*", a sinking feeling grew in my stomach. I understood that a low altitude was the method kamikazes used to hide from radar. Evidently, they were not low enough to evade Harry's Hobert in the radar room. We also knew that our boys generally had no reason to fly that low. All indications pointed to the fact that we were about to be pounded by another suicide attack. My adrenalin was in overdrive as I scanned the sky for any trace of the enemy vermin. I had studied the intricate differences of the Japanese aircraft. I could distinguish the nuances in the sound of the engines. I taught myself to recognize the shape of the fuselage, cockpits, and wings. The trial by fire on the evening of 21 February gave me a lesson on the stench of the exhaust. Although I was not sure if I could claim to have been able to smell them in time to give sufficient warning. That stench is still burned in my memory even today along with the images of their damage to our convoy.

With the general quarters horns howling, all of our boys streaked to their stations. Verlin sprang into his pointer seat while his crew loaded the 40mm rounds. Bill Schorer made ready on his 20mm gun on port side while Jim Romano leapt to his 20mm on starboard. The familiar click-click of the magazines on the twin 20s rang up to the conn.

Ensign Juliana ordered us to cease circling and hold our

bearing dead ahead. His thinking was to make ourselves a smaller target if we met them head on. We waited, and sure enough, five more Japs appeared from the clouds bearing down on our position. All of our guns opened fire at once as well as the guns from the LST-943 positioned just ahead of us to starboard. Verlin at gun number one fired off four 40mm rounds as guns number two, four, and five spewed eighty-nine rounds collectively at the squadron of Zekes. The first plane was struck by the 40mm gun of the LST. The tip of the right wing was severed off and hurled into the water. The plane veered out of control at the ship barely missing the bow. When it neared the water, it began to cartwheel from tail to wing to nose and exploded into a fiery ball.

I saw our guns hit the second with a 40mm round and scores of 20mm rounds peppering the side and wings damaging the ailerons and all stabilizing controls. The wounded plane's engine sputtered as it struggled to suck fuel from the severed lines. Buzz-zut-zut....buzz-zut-zut was the alternating, suffocating sound of the engine. The propeller seemed to be keeping in time with the starting and stopping of the engine. With one last attempt to salvage his mission, the pilot banked toward our stern. With damaged ailerons, the maimed aircraft refused to cooperate with the pilots desperate yanking of the stick and it barrel-rolled out of control into the water with a monstrous eruption of fire and steel.

The other three Jap planes split up to try to divide our

collective fire and selected a ship in its gun sights. Each made strafing runs on our convoy without success except for insignificant pings against the side of the ships and the pitter patter across the water. Ensign Julianna ordered the LSM-143 hard to port at thirty degrees to bring the starboard 20mm guns broad side to the attackers. We were small, so we could turn relatively fast. One of the remaining Zeroes flashed over our conning tower as I ducked in an involuntary reaction. I felt the wind from the racing aircraft and caught a whiff of the oily exhaust. When I glanced back up to the fading sound of the aircraft, it nosed up with its engine straining to gain altitude. Suddenly, it banked left, and as it began its descent, it gathered momentum, and made another run on us. As the aircraft leveled, the pilot squeezed off a round of 7.7mm machine gun fire perfectly timed through the propeller and 20mm cannon fire from the wings. Before he could deliver enough rounds to matter, our 20mm guns tore into his wing. He made a last evasive move over our bow, pulled back hard on his stick, and disappeared into the clouds. The others took hits from all the flak and faded from view. I'm not sure what happened to them. Maybe they were going to search the waters for a less lethal target to menace. I scanned the skies once more to make sure they were gone. The best that I could figure was that the remaining zeros were the escorts that always accompanied the kamikaze attacks. The only report they could take back to their base today was that we had blasted two of them out of the sky with no damage to American ships.

When the last plane disappeared from view, Verlin threw off his helmet and exclaimed with elation,

"I got him! I got that dirty Jap!"

Bill yelled from his 20mm,

"Hey Verlin! You had a little help from us!"

Verlin leaned with his elbows on the edge of his turret and smiled. He cupped his hands over his mouth so that the entire crew could hear and retorted,

"Oh, sorry Bill, I didn't know you were back there!"

All Bill could do was shake his head and laugh. He enjoyed Verlin's comedy as much as the rest of us, and just took the comments in stride. It was a job well done. I gained a real appreciation for those boys on that day. We were pretty deadly for a little two hundred foot tub, and we were NOT going to be left holding our fire this time.

We remained under Condition One Mike for the next twenty minutes and at 1551 hours we were secured from general quarters. This was twice in as many days that I had been nearly brushed by a Jap plane. I could have almost reached up and touched the underbelly of the beast. Almost. I felt like I had been swimming with sharks. One came at us and swam away, then other. We commenced to make our circles in the night retirement area while we awaited orders to deliver the Marines and their equipment to Green Beach.

The Unrelenting Menace

Operation Detachment (D-Day+4): On 23 February, 0807
hours, we were asked to tow the LCM KA-91-3 back to its
mother ship the KA-91. The waters had been so rough that the
LCM (Landing Craft, Mechanized) could not make it back
safety under its own power. The LCM that we were towing
was the fourth generation (LCM(4)) with a length of fifty feet
and an empty displacement of twenty-three tons. The LCM
was designed to haul either one thirty-ton tank or sixty troops
to shore. Maximum capacity for this little boat was sixty
thousand pounds. It was not designed to be an open ocean
ship. It was simply a boat that required a mother ship as
transport across the ocean. However, the newly designed
LCM(4) was fitted with special ballast tanks that allowed for
better stability than its predecessors. We had to tie up to this
little boat and give it some assistance back to its dock on the
KA-91. At about 1020 hours, we heard the entire fleet
sounding their fog horns like there was a traffic jam at rush
hour. I looked back at the island to see a small American flag
waving at the top of "*Hot Rocks*". It was what would have
been later known as the "*first flag raising*". It was a beautiful
sight! The "*second flag raising*", occurring approximately two
hours later, was made famous by the photographer Joe
Rosenthal. The photo of the second flag raising graced the
front page of all the newspapers back home, and is said to have
been a pivotal moment in boosting morale back home. Ensign
Juliana joined in on the fog horn blast with some of his own.

When we saw the flag, it really heightened the resolve of the entire fleet. It made us proud to be a part of this operation. I didn't get to witness the raising of either flag. But, it was a glorious symbol to glance toward every time we made a landing. Hope is hard to come by in war. That solitary flag gave us hope.

By 1045 hours we were lying in wait in what was codenamed as *"Transport Area Baker"*, approximately fifteen thousand yards southeast of the island. During the opening days of the invasion, most of our loading operations were performed in this area to avoid enemy shelling from the shore. We had maintained that position until it was time to return to the night retirement area at 1840 hours to continue our frothy rings.

Every night the Japs had control of the skies. The Japs were always shelling and attacking our Marines on the beach. The Marines were getting it from machine guns and stuff ahead of them, and we were getting it from overhead. At dusk, the night sky was still dimly lit, and it was getting to the point to where small nuances were all that could be seen in the distance. The water reflected the orange hues from the evening sun barely peeking through the cloudy sky. In the mix were the purple and gray clouds ominously hanging directly overhead. I could still see the waves distort the mirror image of the clouds from above. Two thousand yards off our port bow was the LST-944. We stayed at this distance to keep out of friendly fire and to make more difficult targets for Nip bombers and kamikazes.

At 1958 hours, our radar room reported one unidentified aircraft on a course bearing 115 degrees relative at a very high altitude. This placed the aircraft to our starboard quarter, and heading in our direction. With the fall of dusk over the convoy, it was very difficult to spot enemy aircraft. The higher altitude was somewhat puzzling which made me optimistic that it could be one of our boys. But, once he emerged into view, I pressed general quarters as soon as I saw the red dots on the wings and the cigar-like shape of the fuselage. It had the silhouette of the nighttime Jap bomber we had nicknamed the "*Betty*" (*Mitsubishi G4M*). It was still light enough for me to tell that the aircraft was not one of ours.

The Allies and even the Japanese had uncomplimentary nicknames for this hapless bomber. The Japanese enjoyed the long range, speed, and maneuverability of the G4M, but loathed the apparent lack of armor protecting the crew and the wing-borne fuel tanks. Japanese crews even coined nicknames such as a *hamaki* (translated: "*cigar*") while the Allies used "*one-shot lighter*" and "*flying Zippo*". The Betty's positive attributes were due in part to the light design of the aircraft. In earlier versions of the plane, there was no crew compartment armor or self-sealing fuel tanks that later versions comprised.

This made the Betty and its crew almost effortless victims of anti-aircraft and Allied fighters. It was reported that if a gunner could strike the fuel tanks in the wings, the G4M would immediately be engulfed by flames. Our 40mm pointer, Verlin Smith, was privy to that information because I had heard him brag of the fact. He had also claimed to have known the vulnerabilities of the Zero and the Oscar. He explained that if you could hit the Zero (*Mitsubishi A6M*) or the Oscar (*Nakajima Ki-43*) just aft of the canopy and where the wings join the fuselage, you would hit the gas tank and the aircraft would burn and the wings would fly off. I just brushed this talk off as "bull" until after I had witnessed the actions from the last few days. Either way, I had hoped that he was right this time too.

The conning tower of an LSM is on the starboard quarter of the ship which left me looking up at this plane on a course to be directly overhead in a matter of seconds. When Verlin knew the aircraft was in range, he opened fire from his twin-forty on the bow. Then, without hesitation, our twin-twenties commenced. Once the LST-944 saw that we had fired upon the bomber, her guns began to spit lead. They were all firing at once with every third shell as a tracer. At dusk, one was only seeing a third of bullets because you could only see the tracers. Wow! The sight was just fantastic! They were just arching up like fireflies in a race. As the plane arrived directly overhead the ominous whistle of bombs filled the night sky. I, once again, took cover and prayed for God's protection. There is absolutely no place to hide on the conning tower. I was completely exposed. I reasoned that if I could duck down it would be like crouching in a foxhole. These bombs were coming straight down. I didn't have a prayer if the bombardier was good at his job. A Betty's bomb bay was usually loaded with four 500-pound bombs. The whistling sound does not give any clue as to how many, but Ensign Juliana had written in our deck log that three had been jettisoned from the plane that night. Thankfully, the bombardier of that Betty had misjudged its target and the bombs fell harmlessly seven hundred fifty feet to our port beam. We had been overshot, or the LST-944 had been undershot! Ensign Eugene C Bowden aboard the LST wrote in their deck log that the bombs had fallen fifteen hundred yards off the ship's starboard quarter. The bombs fell much closer to us, so I have to believe that we were the intended target. Another great reason that it was good to be small. The concussion from the explosions knocked some of the guys in the engine room off their feet from the shock. I could feel the entire ship shutter as I clung to the edge of the conn. The explosive power of those five hundred pounders was just frightening. They were trying to put us out of commission, but to an airplane, we were a pretty small target and a moving target, of course. It didn't work with us, but they came close enough.

During the entire melee; Verlin, Bill, and the others never

let up. They spun their turrets around and followed the aircraft with their deadly projectiles and tracers. Our 40mm gun made a direct hit on just that sweet spot on the wing. It was one thing to brag about it, but Verlin learned to lead the aircraft so that it would run into the rounds. It was the way fighter pilots were taught to fire in front of the target to allow the enemy to meet the path of the bullets. He was THAT good. In an instant, the aircraft ignited into a fireball sending metal and flames in all directions. Every piece of that aircraft rained down into the waves just to the port side of the LST-944. I could see a sliver of the wing that had the red Japanese insignia on the side still bobbing on the surface. The current swept it farther and farther across the horizon until it disappeared completely from view. With the gray overcast sky, the view of objects on the water's surface was not "glared away" by the sun. Our gun crew took claim for shooting down that Jap plane that day. Our boys on the guns took that Jap out! We proudly painted a Japanese flag on the conning tower for each of the two enemy planes we downed those past couple of days. We never thought too much about it at the time, but if we could fire our anti-aircraft, one ship was not much of a threat to an airplane. But we proved that with all of our guns blazing, we could be lethal.

As soon as garrison aircraft could be accommodated at south field Iwo, they flew in from Saipan. The first were Army

P-51 Mustang day fighters and the P-61 Black Widow night fighters which arrived on 6 March, and took over local day and night combat air patrols (CAP). Two days later more P-51s and a squadron of Avengers from the Marine Torpedo Bomber group (VMTB) arrived. By 11 March, all air activity at Iwo was provided by shore-based aircraft operating from the captured field. On that same day, the last of the air craft carriers were withdrawn to support the upcoming invasion of Okinawa. We were real happy when news came down that the Army brought the P-61 Black Widows. We felt more secure. It put an end to the night time bombing because now WE ruled the sky. The F4U Corsairs, and the newly arrived P-51 Mustangs, were still the kings of the skies during the day. However, the P-61 Black Widow reigned over the night.

The Northrop P-61 was the first aircraft equipped with IFF radar and a remote controlled machine gun turret that could be operated by the radarman or a gunner. In the nose was a rotating radar antenna that emitted microwaves that were reflected from aircraft that found itself within five miles of the Black Widow. It was the first to be built from the ground up as a "night fighter". The technology had been added and used successfully on the F6F Hellcat, but the P-61 was the first to be designed from drawing board to combat zone for nighttime operations. The engineering was developed from what the US had learned from the RAF's RADAR programs. They knew that a night fighter needed three things: speed, armament, and excellent radar. The P-61 had all three aspects that permitted the aircraft to be a deadly weapon in total darkness. It was equipped with twin Pratt and Whitney R2800 engines giving it a top speed of three hundred sixty-five miles per hour. The Black Widow was armed with four fifty caliber machine guns and four 20mm cannons. Its crew of three included the pilot, gunner, and radar observer. The radar observer utilized two scopes when directing the pilot into firing position. The scope on the right provided the range from the enemy and the scope on the left imparted the elevation off the nose. Though it appeared clumsy at first glance, pilots raved over the agility and responsiveness of the aircraft. Because of its effectiveness in neutralizing the enemy, the Black Widow quickly became synonymous with night fighting. These P-61s were part of the 548th and 549th Night Fighter Squadrons assigned to the area to neutralize the Japanese "Betty" bombers looming over the waters near Iwo Jima. Just like its namesake implies, the Black Widow injected its venom and devoured its prey.

Operation Detachment (D-Day+7): LSTs and LSMs were sent to the beaches as soon as the beachhead was secured. These, too, had difficulty avoiding broaching the shore. Several failed when anchors did not hold. Tugs were in constant attendance to tow them clear. Unloading continued day and night with the beach parties working around the clock. Ships of the Gunfire and Covering Force delivered call fire missions during the day and starshell illumination fire throughout the night. These support ships were positioned along the edges of the transport area in order to properly deliver the fire required to keep the Japanese artillery at bay. The unprecedented need for so much call fire was due to the restrictive effect of the weather upon air support, and to the enemy's strong resistance.

The day after the bombing, the OTC (Officer of Tactical Command) was transferred from LST-944 to LST-646. Therefore, from the night retirement area we transferred to the Transport Area Baker to assume our position astern the LST-646 awaiting our orders to land our men and equipment. We remained in Area Baker until 0536 hours, Monday, 26 February when we were ordered to proceed to Green Beach I. When we arrived at our landing zone, we had to wait close to an hour for LST-247 to clear the beach. Our initial landing at Iwo Jima involved deploying tanks, trucks filled with flame-thrower fuel, and other equipment with a rendezvous point at Green Beach I. Green Beach I was the point closest to the base of Mount Suribachi at which the first and second battalions of the 28th Marine Regiment had landed on D-Day. The Marine Engineers that we had on board were to go ashore to build a road to the top of Mt. Suribachi on D-Day plus seven; 26 February. We only had one tank; we had room for more than one, but we had several trucks loaded with gear. We had men, Marines, that I never saw leave the ship. I had my own thing to take care of. I never actually saw the Marines running ashore, but they did. The voice over the loudspeaker called the Marines to the deck:

"Now hear this. Now hear this.

All troops report to your debarking stations.

All troops report to your debarking stations."

We had sounded general quarters and were under Condition One Mike for all hands to be at battle stations. It was a trip to shore that seemed like an eternity. At 0804 hours, we had turned to the beach and ordered all engines ahead full. With a full load and a low draft that only meant that we were steaming at around eight or nine knots. The shells from the battleships whizzed overhead like freight trains on a collision course. These shells were on a target for areas beyond the front lines. When they hit the island off in the distance, it SOUNDED like a crashing freight train. The salvo was deafening. The shelling was relentless. The cacophony suggested the end of the world. To our port was the infamous Mount Suribachi. It was an ominous figure that jetted upward from the southwest corner of the island. It personified a sea monster poking its head above the surf for a look at its next victim. The Japs seemed to be as much dedicated in firing on the cargo ships in the water as they were on the ones making the landing on the beach. As I stared at the beach, it looked like a smoldering fire pit. It was like a campfire looks when all the wood is gone and all that is left is the ash and smoke. I just stared at it. I stared at it like I was

looking for the answers to why we were here. That answer
would never come to me. It didn't come to me at that moment
anyway. I caught myself slowly scanning the entire island in

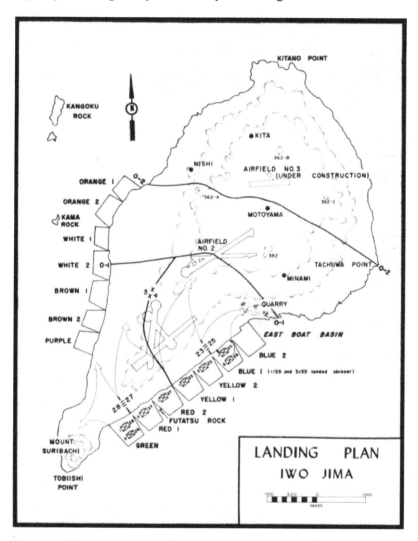

disbelief.

The outlines of the men in drab green uniforms sprawled
out on the beach. I had to look away for a moment and get my
head back into place. Along the beach, I could see the

corpsmen tending to them, and the stretcher bearers loading the wounded onto landing ships to take them back to the hospital vessels. DUKWs, LCMs, and LCVPs were lying in capsized, burned heaps. Many of the vessels were half buried in the loose, black, volcanic ash. It couldn't be called sand. It was just a buildup of years and years of volcanic activity resulting in a kind of mush. Neither men nor machine were any better off on the beach than on the front lines. Nevertheless, they had to come to the beach for transport aboard incoming landing vessels. I stared down at the floor of the conn for a moment and muttered to myself:

"You have a job to do, Garforth! Get it together!"

As we approached five hundred fifty feet from shore, we let go the stern anchor allowing it to trail out behind us as it dug into the oceans bottom. We had done this a hundred times at San Clemente, San Diego, Pyramid Cove, and Little Creek. This was for real, and yet it was surreal. It was like it was happening to someone else, and I was watching one of those John Wayne movies on our movie projector below deck. This time, it wasn't just our boys dropping the lead; it was coming in our direction as well. As we got within a few hundred feet, the machine gun slugs began to ping against the hull of the 143. I said a short, silent word to God for the safety of the Marines in the well deck and our boys on board. As quick as I could say "amen", our bow began to rise and the bottom scraped across the soft, black sand.

"Load and lock gentlemen!"

I heard the commanding officer of the Marines yell just before the bow doors opened and the ramp lowered. I couldn't watch them exit, so I kept myself busy getting prepared to signal the AKA from which we were about to offload our next load. I could hear the fifty calibers dot the side of the ship.

We had to keep our engines ahead in order to keep the stern of the ship from broaching. The sand was so loose on Iwo Jima that the stern anchor could not get a firm enough grip on the ocean's bottom. The adverse beach conditions were apparent the entire time we were beached. With a steep gradient such as this, the surf breaks directly upon the beach. It was impossible with the heavy swells for many of the smaller landing craft like the DUKWs and Higgins boats to keep from broaching. With each wave, boats were picked up bodily and thrown broadside to the beach where succeeding waves swamped and wrecked them. Losses had to be accepted until the beachhead was secured, and until the LSTs, LSMs, and LCTs could be employed. The resultant accumulation of wreckage piled progressively higher and extended seaward into the beach approaches to form underwater obstacles which damaged propellers and even gutted a few of the LSTs and LSMs.

Although seaweed gave the false appearance that the beach was hard packed, it was soon discovered that the volcanic ash had no cohesive consistency. Wheeled vehicles bogged down to the axles. Even tanks and other tracked vehicles moved with difficulty over the forty percent grade of the beach. Because of these obstacles, a trail of wreckage marked the way.

Once the last of the cargo was unloaded, and the men disembarked, the anchor winch engaged and the engines revved full astern. The ship slowly scraped across the ductile sand. We had gotten stuck momentarily in the quagmire until the engines were ordered to flank speed. We slowly broke free, and wheeled around. As the ship began to straighten, we felt something strike the stern. I looked down into the water to see a submerged Amtrak (*Landing Vehicle Tracked or LVT*). There was no reef around the island that I knew of but we had struck a sunken amphibian with our starboard propeller. Without further hesitation, we weighed anchor and headed out to the AKA in waiting. The order relayed to the engine room

was for engines all ahead flank. That was the only speed we used when we left a landing at Iwo. We had to get the hell out of there, and fast! The Nips weren't just firing small arms;

they had the big stuff too. They were dropping 75mm rounds down on us. There was no time to waste. Not only were we being fired upon, but the sand was a mushy mess that required our engines to be pushed to their utmost limits.

Although we struck a quite a few underwater obstacles on our way to subsequent landings, groups were working feverishly to get the landing zones extricated as quickly as possible. The Underwater Demolition Teams (UDTs) and beach parties freed the beaches and surrounding surf of accumulated wreckage. The UDTs were the predecessor of the modern-day Navy SEALS. The Service and Salvage Group cleared the beach approaches, salvaged boats and pontoons, and affected emergency repairs on damaged ships. These were herculean tasks and proceeded apace with the unloading, the replenishment, the evacuation of casualties, and the rendering of supporting fires so that the assault might continue.

We had learned to let go the stern anchor one hundred feet sooner (six hundred fifty feet from shore) in order to get a good hold with the anchor. This proved to be the best distance for our landings since we had so much difficulty on the first landing at five hundred fifty feet. It was a crap-shoot most of the time so we had to try different things on the different landing zones around the island. If we didn't get a good hold on the beach, we had to us the engines to keep the stern from broaching.

Some of the Marines drove the trucks; some drove tanks.

Our main objective was to get rid of this equipment they loaded on us. Take it in and drop it off at whatever beach they told us. We had continued for several days unloading supplies for the 28th Marines on Green Beach I. During the first few days of March, we unloaded supplies and cargo for the 23rd Marines on Yellow Beach II on the southeast side.

As soon as we got unloaded each time, we backed off the beach, wheeled around, and found the APA or AKA to reload. We'd go alongside; I would signal to them with my light and

The stern of the LSM-143 barely visible in this photo at the beach on Iwo Jima

make arrangements. It was my job to signal the mother ship just before we tied up to it. Then, they would offload cargo down into our open well deck. That was our job every day.

Operation Detachment (D-Day+9):   At 0400 hours, 28

February, we were moored alongside AKA-64 in rough waters with heavy swells lifting and pitching both ships. Loading should have been postponed, but we had put off our operations for too long. We HAD to get equipment to the beach. I was shining down into the deck just as I had done the entire time we were at Iwo Jima during nighttime loading. I was also uncomfortably close to the crane that was to load the cargo down into the well deck. We had trucks and equipment to load on this night, and the first thing to load was the truck. It swung back and forth with the rise and fall of the AKA. Out of control, it smashed into Gun #2. This knocked it out of alignment and rendered it useless. Once the crane operator maintained control of the load, he gently lowered it onto our well deck. On the return of the crane to the AKA, the boom inadvertently struck the radar antenna leaving us without radar operations. None of this had been the fault of the crane operator. We were all at the mercy of the rough seas during much of our operations. We figured that we had enough fire power remaining to protect ourselves, and we could rely on Eldon in the radio room for communications regarding warnings. This would have to suffice until we could get someone to work on the radar. We untied from AKA-64 and made way at full speed to Green Beach I. It was a pretty close call for me, but I found that I was perched close to the action most of the time. I'm very surprised that the conning tower didn't take any damage that day or any other day for that matter.

Operation Detachment (D-Day+11): 2 March, 0715 hours, we were moored alongside the AKA-90 (USS Whiteside) to load supplies for the 28th Marines. We had moved loading operations closer to shore at approximately eight thousand yards south of the landing zones in an area codenamed *"Transport Area Zebra" (see diagram)*. At the time, the fleet was engaged in a heavy shell bombardment in support of the Marines and to hopefully keep the Japs from interfering with our loading operations. One time, I came really close to getting hit right in the face with shrapnel. The Japanese were said to have been using the Type 41 75mm Mountain Gun to fire from Mount Suribachi out into the water at the cargo ships. The gun had a range of over 4 miles and could easily reach the vessels offloading onto our landing ships.

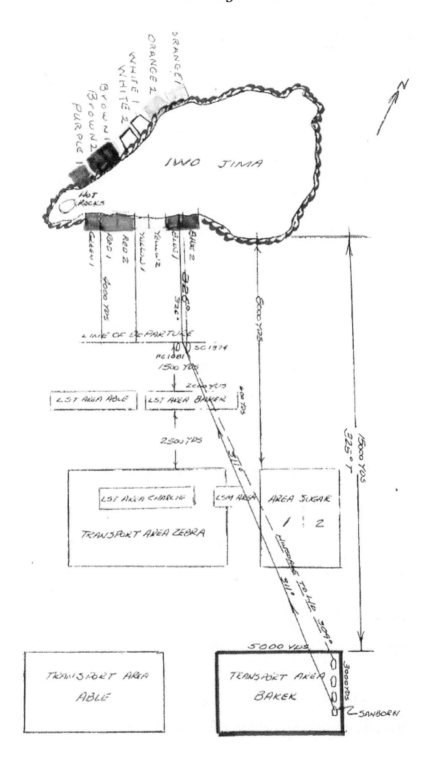

General Quarters!

We were taking on cargo from the cranes of the AKA-90, when all of the sudden, these small boats were running out from shore. It dawned on me that it was kind of strange that these ships were all going out at the same time. By the time the loading was almost complete, it was around 1845 hours and relatively dark. My flood lamp was pretty big and powerful that I had shining down on our deck. They had their winch extended down into our deck lowering a piece of artillery. With us being in the Northern Pacific in the winter time, it was cold out there. I was on my elbows on the rim of the conning tower with my face right up against the shell of the light to benefit from its glowing warmth. It was like I had done as a boy at my Grandpa's house huddling next to his big pot belly stove on a cold February day in Michigan.

There was quite a bit of shelling coming from the Japs' artillery on shore. Their plan was to take out the supply ships before we could unload from them. Suddenly there was this flash in the rigging on the AKA that we were unloading. Then there was a big explosion near the top of the rigging. The ping of shrapnel rang on the opposite side of my light. The deck went dark, and glass from the light went everywhere. I leaped back from the light just as it went black. I thought I had been hit and so did the officer on deck Ensign Julianna.

"Garforth! Are you alright?" Ensign Julianna exclaimed with a look of horror on his face. He must have thought that I had taken a hit. He was as white as a sheet, and I'm sure that I

had a similar expression.

I frantically checked by face, arms, and torso. I thought to myself, *"Oh my God! Maybe I'm dead! I don't feel any pain."*

As soon as I came to my senses, I punched the general quarters button. All the officers and crew came running to their stations. Later, we got a chance to examine and found a dent on the shell of the light and a piece of shrapnel about as big as a man's fist lying inside. If it wasn't for that light, I would have been killed. Furthermore, if my head had been resting on the other side, it would have invariably been my end. I'm not sure what kind of damage the AKA-90 took during that barrage. As far as I could tell, no one was hurt by the blast. By 1830 hours, we untied and headed to our assigned landing zone with what we had loaded.

Operation Detachment (D-Day+12/13): As the days wore on, we had motored between Transport Area Zebra and various landing zones for the past couple of days. 3 March, 1825 hours, found us moored in "Zebra" along the starboard side of the USS Starr (AKA-67) while the LSM-207 was moored to port. We remained in this position until 4 March at 0215 hours when the LSM-207 cast off. The AKA-67 commenced to loading our cargo including one tank dozer, a flamethrower fuel tanker, and a platoon of twenty-one Marines. By 0545 hours, we were loaded and underway to our landing zone on Yellow Beach II. With all the amphibious traffic parked on the beach, we had to wait until 0851 hours to begin our landing sequence.

We landed, open the bow doors, lowered the ramp and machine gun slugs started flying around. The Japs had a tunnel, a little cave right there on the beach, and as soon as we landed, they opened fire. The guns must have been .50 caliber or so because the bullets made some indentations into the side of the well deck. We laughed about it later, but we had this African-American boy by the name of Willie Washington. His duty

was telephone talker for the number one turret, so he was on the main deck. He was caught down on the bow of the ship at a really bad time. We had a tank with a bulldozer blade on the front that was in the lead. Each tank company was assigned two dozer kits, which could be mounted as needed to create these "tankdozers". Tankdozers proved to be quite valuable in that they could bury heavily defended enemy emplacements under a thick layer of dirt. The tank commander was standing up in his open turret, and was fully exposed from about the waist up. Willie knew what was going on; they were shooting at him! He jumped behind the blade. Well, the tank commander didn't know Willie was down there, so he raised the bulldozer blade to protect himself. We were taking it all in from the bridge. The captain hollered down from the conn;

"Willie, get the hell outta there!"

Willie opened his eyes and could see what had happened. He was lying on the deck, fully exposed. He got to his feet, and made a streak along the full length of the deck and got out of harm's way. It wasn't funny at the time, but later on it was kind of funny. We were ribbing Willie, really giving him the business.

Operation Detachment (D-Day+14-22): Every day was just like clockwork. A huge crane from an APA or AKA would load cargo into our open well deck, we would slide onto a landing zone, unload, heave back off the beach, and repeat. This would happen two or three times a day depending on the cargo. Most of our landings during this period were at Yellow and Blue beaches. We had even been sent on the west side to Purple Beach which was just as close to Suribachi as Green Beach on the east side.

Directly across from Yellow Beach on the southwest side of the island was Purple Beach which was adjacent to Brown Beach to the north. Purple Beach was just a mirror image of

Green Beach I in that we were still in sight of Mount Suribachi. In the last week of February, the Hydrographic Survey Group completed a survey for locating mooring buoys and nets. It had been noted that, as long as easterly winds prevailed, the resultant swells continued to make conditions difficult on the eastern beaches. The front lines had advanced sufficiently to indicate the feasibility of a shift to the western beaches. Consequently, a survey of Purple and Brown beaches commenced. It was found that these beaches would be excellent for boats, but that the water was too shallow for craft larger than an LSM. The situation indicated that these beaches could best be used initially for unloading ammunition; and plans for creating exits ashore from these beaches proceeded accordingly.

While moving from cargo ship to shore, we were bound to have grazed a few obstacles just below the water's surface. Although no particular strikes were obvious at the time, detecting such bumps were overshadowed by the roughness of the surf as we were steaming ashore. Propellers can take a few bumps against objects in the water, but not as many as we had taken at Iwo Jima.

On 8 March the starboard engine had slowed from 450 RPM to 275 during a beaching order. The engine room halted the engines and we filled the wing ballast tanks to keep from broaching while we were beached. Filling the ballast tanks kept our draft down low enough so that our hull would rest against the sand in an attempt to keep our stern straight. To troubleshoot our problem with the starboard engine, Lieutenant Merschel requested mechanics from the USS Agenor (ARL-3).

We emptied the ballast, and retracted from the beach to meet the ARL-3 in an anchorage for repairs. After extensive testing on the afternoon of 9 March, the mechanics found no problems with the engine and suggested that we have someone inspect the propellers. Both engines had shown signs of overheating which indicated that the sea chest could have been clogged. The sea chest was a water collecting reservoir with an intake just below the water's surface to supply the engines with cooling water and for fresh water conversions.

By 0907 hours on 10 March, divers arrived aboard an LCM to examine the condition of our props. Within just moments, one of the divers surfaced to inform Ensign Juliana that a cargo net had been caught and wound around both propellers. The divers also discovered that the grating over the sea chest had been almost completely clogged. The sea chest was sucking in all of this debris that our landing operations had been kicking up. They had found seaweed blocking the outside of the screens and the nasty black volcanic ash up in the reservoir. It was just a matter of time before the port engine would have felt the effects. The divers spent the next twelve minutes cutting the cargo net from the screws. Cargo net entanglement was a common occurrence with over half of the LSMs in the fleet. We were never sure if the cargo nets had been discarded or somehow accidentally lost, but they ended up washing near the shore.

While the divers were submerged, they also cleared the grating of the sea chest as much as possible. When they surfaced for the final time, we were informed that the propellers would need to be replaced as soon as we could get to a dry dock. The grating from the sea chest would have to be removed and more extensive cleaning would be required. They had also assessed the damage to the hull and found massive scarring from our landings that could possibly lead to leaks.

For the next two days we loaded and unloaded cargo to Yellow Beach II while we awaited an opening in the next dry dock. It was like waiting for the doctor. We just went along our operations like nothing was wrong with the ship. The LSM-143 motored like a champ. We just knew that it was running on borrowed time. At 1505 hours on 12 March we had unloaded from Yellow Beach II and made preparations to proceed to the vicinity of the USS Belle Grove (LSD-2) in the eastern anchorage. By 1620 hours, we were given docking instructions as we watched the LSD-2 fill its ballast tanks to sink far enough for us to drive into its dock. Once we were in position, the LSD-2 emptied its ballast tanks and the LSM-143 settled onto the Belle Grove's deck. The crew wasted no time in welding repair patches to our hull to cover the damage made by our ceaseless landings. Simultaneously, the crew began work on replacing both propellers and cleaning out the sea chest. They worked well into the night and by 0600 the next morning, our ship had received all needed repairs.

The dry dock flooded itself by filling the ballast tanks and, by 0700 hours, we were water borne and underway to receive a full tank of diesel fuel from the USS Cache (AO-67). Not only had our hull and screws been spent, but so had our fuel supply. The LSM-143 was healed with a full belly, and ready for action.

On the sixteenth, we were moored alongside the USS William C Ralston to take on cargo and equipment assigned to be delivered to Blue Beach I. This time we had a different kind of cargo accompanying us. The 28th Marine Division Field Hospital was located near Blue Beach I and we were asked to take a wounded Marine on our way. "Doc" Mallchok took care of the private's wounds until we could get him to the hospital. When we landed on Blue Beach I on the morning of 17 March, PFC PD Talley was the first "cargo" to be taken from the ship that day. Three of our boys assisted "Doc" in carrying the stretcher off the ramp and onto a troop truck waiting on shore. It was sobering to watch a Marine carried from our ship when we had seen so many running off the ramp. However, it was comforting to know that he was going to be alright.

Throughout the remainder of March and until 9 April, the LSM-143 participated in landing operations at Iwo Jima. We had been informed that the beach had been officially pronounced secured by the Marines on 26 March. This was following a horrific, final banzai attack reportedly lead by Kuribayashi himself. When the battle came to an end over ninety minutes later, fifty-three Americans were killed and one hundred twenty wounded. This number included Army pilots, Seabees, and Marines.

On the morning of 27 March, we had orders to transport Marines from the island to the AKA-117. I just figured it would be a platoon or two with some equipment. When we got there, I saw what looked like an entire company of Marines. We landed on the beach and lowered the ramp while nine hundred fifty haggard, "raggedy", Marines trudged into our well deck. They were a worn out looking crew with torn, filthy dungarees. It was hard to imagine what those boys had been through. The entire company packed into our well deck, and within twenty-five minutes of the landing, we retracted. We met the USS Zaurek (AKA-117) in the western anchorage. We pulled alongside the Zaurek where they had already had the cargo net draped over the side. With weary muscles, each man pulled himself up the cargo net like ants up a hill. I'm sure it was a hollow reminder of what they had endured over a month ago. Even as tired as they appeared, they scaled that net like it was nothing. Within forty minutes, all nine hundred fifty Marines were on board the AKA-117 for some well-deserved rest and hot chow.

Farther north toward the Japanese mainland, landing forces had delivered Marines and equipment for the invasion of Okinawa (*Operation Iceberg*) on D-Day, 1 April 1945. It would be Easter Sunday and April Fool's Day all in one. The fighting would prove to be just as brutal as that on Iwo Jima, and the Kamikaze attacks magnified a hundred times.

By 9 April, we had covered every single beach on the east and west side of Iwo Jima at one time or another. The last time we landed, 6 April, we stayed on White Beach I when the island had been somewhat secured. They had big concrete pill boxes and gun emplacements all along the beach. We were pretty much on our own on the beach. We really weren't supposed to be there because the island wasn't known to be totally secured. Anyway, I remember, a couple of my shipmates and I were not very far off the beach, practically in the water's edge. We saw this pill box that had been put out of commission, and we looked in. It had been blown up but, the roof was still good. We could see a bunch of dead Japs in there. We saw one Jap, he was minus his legs from the knees down; he was minus his arms; he was on all fours with his uniform blown off or burned off, I don't know. We said to each other, "*Boy, there's a good Jap*". It didn't really hit until later when I got to thinking about what I had seen. I really didn't have time to worry about something else at the time. Now that I have had years to reflect, I am remorseful for both sides when I discuss the events of this horrible battle on this tiny island. There was so much sacrifice for such a meager real estate.

Chapter 11

SHE WAS A CASUALTY OF WAR

On 31 March 1945 Rear Admiral H.W. Hill recommended a unit citation for the actions of LSM Group Fourteen during the Iwo Jima campaign. Admiral Hill was the commanding and second in command of the Joint Expeditionary Force (Task Force 53), comprising an air support control unit, two transport squadrons, tractor groups, LSM groups, control groups, beach party groups, LCT groups, with the mission of transporting and landing the expeditionary troops. The citation read as follows:

"I wish to commend you and your group most highly for your outstanding achievement at Iwo Jima. Despite the tremendous difficulties and hazards involved the response of LSMs to operational orders was immediate and their performance was of the highest order. They contributed materially to the success of the entire operation. Please convey to all concerned my sincere appreciation for their excellent service.

I am intensely proud of you. You performed an outstanding job in the face of extreme difficulties and severe handicaps. You kept your ships operating ceaselessly night and day in spite of their damaged and battered condition. You persevered in the face of heavy enemy fire in spite of the most adverse beaching conditions. You successfully landed your cargo on one of the bloodiest beacheads in the Pacific. You did an excellent job."

Unhesitatingly, I have recommended you for the Unit Citation."

Signed,

Albert E Lind

```
                         LSM GROUP FOURTEEN
LSM GR. 14/P15              FLOTILLA FIVE
19                       C/O FLEET POST OFFICE
                         SAN FRANCISCO, CALIF.


                                        31 March 1945


From:     Commander, LSM Group FOURTEEN, Flotilla FIVE.
To:       LSM Group FOURTEEN, All Hands.

Subject:  Commendation for the Iwo Jima Campaign.

     1.        The following despatch was received by this command from
Rear Admiral HILL, Commander Task Force 53, Iwo Jima operation.

"I WISH TO COMMEND YOU AND YOUR GROUP MOST HIGHLY FOR YOUR OUTSTANDING
ACHIEVEMENT AT IWO JIMA X DESPITE THE TREMENDOUS DIFFICULTIES AND HAZARDS
INVOLVED THE RESPONSE OF LSMS TO OPERATIONAL ORDERS WAS IMMEDIATE AND THE
PERFORMANCE WAS OF THE HIGHEST ORDER X THEY CONTRIBUTED MATERIALLY TO THE
SUCCESS OF THE ENTIRE OPERATION X PLEASE CONVEY TO ALL CONCERNED MY SINCERE
APPRECIATION FOR THEIR EXCELLENT SERVICE"

     2.        I am intensely proud of you. You performed an outstanding job
in the face of extreme difficulties and severe handicaps. You kept your
ships operating ceaselessly night and day in spite of their damaged and
battered condition. You perservered in the face of heavy enemy fire and in
spite of the most adverse beaching conditions. You successfully landed
your cargo on one of the bloodiest beacheads in the Pacific. You did an
excellent job.

          Unhesitatingly, I have recommended you for the Unit Citation.


                         ALBERT E. LIND




Ensign James Nicholas Juliana
LSM 145
```

Generally, we didn't land on the beaches at night. We would stay on the beach overnight while the cargo was being unloaded. The ship needed to be landed during daylight hours in order for us to judge the best angle of approach. However, we spent many evenings moored to an APA or an AKA loading aboard cargo or troops before we would go into night retirement to await enough daylight to make a successful landing. We didn't get much sleep because we were constantly at general quarters or we were at our duty stations. The weather was bad the entire time, so we had to deal with heavy swells, rain, and rough surf. The commendation was a very nice gesture. It proved to us that the job we were doing was not being overlooked. I think all us boys on board were so busy doing the things that we were supposed to do that we didn't look upon it as out of the ordinary.

It took a toll on the ship much worse than on the sailors. The roughness of the beach and being moored so closely to the cargo ships during rough seas caused heavy hull damage. Several accidental collisions during crane operations damaged one of our 20mm guns, the radar antennae, and countless other items on board. The sea chest became clogged so badly with beach debris that it eventually caused the engines to overheat. As a result, the starboard engine failed causing us to perform several landings with just the aid of the port engine. The propellers took damage from striking reefs and other underwater obstacles during landings. I will never forget the searchlight that we lost in an artillery barrage. The ship took on so much punishment that it eventually became a casualty of war. The after action report detailed all the damages throughout the ship. The following is the exact wording in the report:

*"Exhaust fan housing crushed, galley fan housing crushed, engine room upper level exhaust fan housing crushed, two diesel oil fill lines broken off, generator diesel oil day tank bent off of bulkhead, port main engine diesel oil day tank bent from bulkhead, valve to fill generator diesel day tank inoperative hydraulic coupling pressure relief line broken at welded flange, drill press table out of alignment, machine shop power panel bent in on bulkhead, battery charging panel broken loose from bulkhead, tool cabinet bent from wall, drain line from fire main broken off, gasoline barrel holding apparatus broken, mufflers in both generators breaking through and rotting, **sea chest badly clogged due to running on beach and in excessive debris**, forward and aft fire main connections broken off at deck, four battery charging panels bent and battered, bad shaft vibration port at starboard speed 600 RPM, fire hydrants at frames 15 and 25 port side damaged, life lines and stanchions on port side and aft are damaged, boat davit and socket damaged, life raft stanchions damaged, both port ventilators damaged, fire hose racks on port side damaged, **ramp cables need replacing (one on port and two on starboard side)**, replace mat, **#2 gun and tub damaged by loading crane**, torn*

*and bent chocks (port side), hole in port side between frame 3 and 5, cracked weld in steering flats (frame 40 port side), **BK radar broken by a boom during loading operations**, **searchlight damaged by enemy shell**, stanchions and stern light on stern damage, bent bulkhead and buckled deck (40mm hydraulic room) also torn welds in the same compartment, frames between 19 and 27 bent in on port side, port bow flap strip damaged, port bulwark badly bent."*

We experienced engine problems off and on since around 8 March. The mechanics would make band-aid repairs and send us on our way. It seemed that the engine trouble just wouldn't go away. The LSM-143 was enroute to Saipan on 9 April at 1657 hours in convoy with LST-761, LST-646, and LSM-260 while being escorted by the minesweeper AM-101 and sub chaser PC-1082. Our starboard engine went out before we could even clear the submarine nets. We took our convoy position astern the LST-646 with only the use of our port engine. We were also still without the aid of our radar. It became obvious that serious damage to the entire ship had occurred and repairs were badly needed. The artillery fire, machine gun slugs, and the havoc that the beach landing had wreaked upon the hull had taken its toll. The high RPMs the engine had to turn over and over again to slide the ship from the sand had stressed its limits.

Engine repairs on Saipan took sixteen days from April

thirteenth to the twenty-eighth. The day we got to Saipan, we had received the solemn news that our commander-in-chief, Franklin Delano Roosevelt, had died the day before of a stroke. We had just placed our "absentee" votes a few months prior in the election that awarded FDR an unprecedented fourth term. It was a total shock to all of us on board. I'm sure it was a devastating blow to the people back home as well. FDR had brought us out of the Depression and lead us through the most horrible conflict in our nation's history. We didn't know very much about this Harry Truman fellow. All we knew was that he had been a captain in the field artillery during World War I. The speculation was buzzing more than ever about what he would do or not do. We would just have to wait and see.

We had limped alongside the rest of the fleet without the starboard engine until 7 May when the port engine failed. Our running mate, LSM-260, was ordered to take us in tow the rest of the way to Pearl. At 0950 hours that morning, they attempted to pass a line to our crew. When that failed, the LSM-260 had to circle around for another pass to our port. This time we received the one and a quarter inch cable and attached it to our towing bridle on the bow. With five hundred sixty feet of cable attached to the stern of the LSM-260, we resumed our passage to Pearl Harbor.

Once again, the ship crossed the International Date Line (*this time east bound and in tow*) to Pearl Harbor on 8 May 1945. The clocks on the ship were changed from minus twelve time zone to plus twelve time zone. This moved the date back one day to 8 May. In essence, Tuesday, 8 May 1945 lasted forty-eight hours. Eldon came out of the radio shack shouting,

"Hitler's dead! The Germans have surrendered! The war's over in Europe!"

We just all dismissed it all as just typical "scuttlebutt". But, Eldon had confirmed the statements as official news from the war department. That was good news for the boys in Europe. We had a pretty bad attitude at the time. We really didn't care if the war with the Germans was over. In our part of the world, the war was NOT over! We still had an enemy that was willing to fight to the last. That meant it would be either the last one of us or the last one of them. We thought the war in the Pacific was never going to end.

Just after one day of towing, the cable had come loose from the stern of the LSM-260 once again. The ship circled back around and tied back up to our bow towing bridle, and in a couple of hours, we were back up to convoy speed. After three days of towing us across the Pacific, the LSM-260 had to give up the task of being our tug boat. The stress had become too much on her engines, and our fleet couldn't afford the time to tow two LSMs into Pearl Harbor. On 10 May, the job was passed to the LST-790 who seemed to pull us with great ease. Just past noon on 15 May, the LST-790 pulled us through the submarine nets and into Pearl Harbor. The tug YTM-129 (USS Ceola) was assigned to take over and tow us into our berthing area. It was wonderful to see this beautiful, picturesque island once again. It was a tropical paradise. This was especially true after we had stared at the grey, black landscapes of Iwo Jima. We had gone from looking at an island from day to day that was totally devoid of plant life to an island teeming with lush green palm trees and singing birds. It was a welcome respite.

We spent the next three days under repairs to fix the radar and various other minor fixes. The crews repaired the power panel for the machine shop. Engine repairs commenced while we were anchored as well as the #2 gun that had been damaged during cargo loading. Divers went below to evaluate any possible damage, and resurfaced with the diagnosis of bent screws. Bent screws and strained engines were typical injuries to all amphibians. It appeared from the outside to be a weak ship. However, if outsiders knew what kind of punishment this little vessel took day in and day out, the need for repairs would be justified. This was especially true in combat situations when we were fired upon and skidding along such rough sands as Iwo Jima. Critics can say what they want about the durability of these little ships, but from a sailor's perspective they were tough!

The YTM-129 tugged us into dry dock for repairs to the hull. Work began on straightening the propellers. Crews were welding at every square inch of the LSM-143. They had to reinforce patches that were made in Saipan and new patches were bonded in areas of the hull not repaired before. The ramp cables were replaced from all the wear and tear of heaving the heavy ramp up and down. The original cables had been in operation on our ship ever since it was commissioned on the east coast. So, they had endured the scores of practice landings that we had gone through in the states as well as the combat landings on Iwo Jima.

After a few quick repairs, the ship left Pearl Harbor on 28 May under its own power. It was a great feeling not to have to depend on another ship. It wasn't good for moral to have another ship pull you into port. We kept the engines at standard speed the entire trip to San Diego to take care that we would make it. Our luck would soon run out. About half way to the mainland, the starboard engine began to vibrate. We were ordered to completely stop the engine and try to make it with the trusty port engine. It was déjà vu all over again.

At 2022 hours 7 June, we passed the China Point Light on San Clemente Island. We were in our old training grounds again. We were elated. Early the next morning, we passed through the submarine nets of San Diego Harbor and moored to Pier #3 at the Naval Repair Base. While the ship was under repairs, all shipmates alternated liberty to visit home or the sights of southern California. At 1630 hours on 9 June, half of the crew was granted twenty days leave. I was included in this first group of freshly liberated sailors. What would I do with twenty days of new found freedom? That question went through my head with the fact that we had just gotten paid.

However, it really wasn't enough to sustain a sailor for twenty days in San Diego.

Before I would take a couple of weeks at home, I decided to roam the streets of the west coast. We were on liberty in San Diego and I was feeling pretty salty. I was an old sea dog, but back then I was at the age that everything was novel. If we were on shore, we were looking for a pinball machine. We were modern, and we were associated with modern surroundings. When we got to San Diego, I had a uniform that wasn't Government Issue. I had one that I had bought in one of the big cities, Chicago maybe. It was made out of surge rather than wool; it was different material anyway. It had dragons on the cuffs. We were supposed to have our cuffs buttoned; we wore them turned back. I also had a scarf around my neck that was folded several times and tied really tight just to be cool. We couldn't improve on the Navy issued shoes much but, according to regulations, they had better be shined. The hat was a regular watch cap that I had folded in and creased. We didn't wear our hats square; we wore it raked over one eye like we were really hepcats. Well, we had met a couple of officers that looked like "ninety-day wonders" and maybe they were. They were ALL Navy. At ANY TIME we were supposed to salute an officer. I mean, there were no two ways about it. If we pass one going in the same direction, we had to say "*by your leave Sir*". That is the only way we could walk any faster than him. Well, anyway, I didn't salute him.

So, when I got passed him, he yelled, *"Hey sailor, where's your salute?"*

I replied defiantly, *"Aw, you're kidding!"*

He was livid and demanded my name and rank.

"Watch your manner! And fix your cover sailor!"

So, my buddy and I just turned really quick, went on and got lost in the crowd. We found a magazine stand sitting in front of a deli and ducked in behind. We gave him enough time to get by our position before we showed our faces. I saw him later investigating every group looking for our whereabouts. He was relentless, but he never found us. If he had, we would have been sitting in a cooler somewhere. That's a real infraction of Navy rules. We weren't necessarily saluting the man; we saluted the uniform for which it stood. Some of us thought that we were too salty, had been under fire, and seen too much. We WERE sailors. We didn't have any respect for those guys that were younger than us who had never been in combat situations. Some of those young guys took their training very seriously. I respect that, but I wasn't about to take orders or a reprimand from an officer fresh out of school.

***

I spent a couple of weeks at home and relished in the familiar surroundings of home and the smell of my mother's cooking. Those were the fastest two weeks of my life, but I savored every moment. My grandpa took Leoma and me to

Lake Michigan for a wonderful summertime picnic. We pulled up in the Model T, and I wanted to cry when I saw the sun reflect off that beautiful, calm water. I ran to the beach as fast as I could, and shed my shoes as soon as I reached the edge of the sand. When I dived into the water, I didn't get the salty taste of the ocean on my lips that I had gotten that day that we took our *"swimming break"* in the Pacific. It was just fresh, cool Lake Michigan water. It was invigorating.

When lunch time came, I wanted to tell grandpa the events I had been through at Iwo and the horrible attacks that I had witnessed. I wasn't about to ruin the mood or cause my family any unnecessary worry. Instead, I chose to just sit and eat my lunch while I enjoyed conversation about things that had happened in Fountain while I was gone. I wanted to know what food was growing good this year in the garden, and how well "my" Model T was running. The war stories could wait; especially the one that lingered in the back of my mind – the one about the upcoming invasion of the Japanese mainland – the one that we all knew was inevitable.

On my final day in Fountain, I left my mom and dad in the same state that I left them a year and nine months earlier. My mom cried and my dad just hugged me for the longest time. He didn't say anything, but he didn't have to. I had learned to read his eyes. He hurt to see me go. My mom grabbed me for a hug and a sorrowful whisper. *"Please be safe Delmor. I'm proud of my sailor. I love you."* Mom reluctantly let me go and began to sob. Before I could let my emotions match my mother's, I grabbed my bag and walked through the screen door. In the driver's seat of the Model T was my grandpa waiting to give me a ride back to the bus stop.

"She'll be OK Del. Me and your dad will keep her busy. She won't have time to worry."

***

I returned from my twenty day leave to find the LSM-143 looking as good as it did the day we boarded from boot camp. By 27 July, the 143 had received major repairs to the engines, keel, superstructure and a new port side at the National City, California shipyard. The hull damage had been neatly repaired with new sheet metal welded to perfection where necessary. Other areas were welded back together where there was minimal damage. Once the welding was complete, the LSM-143 received a fresh coat of paint across the entire hull. The heavy port side damage on the LSM-143 was sustained during the Battle of Iwo Jima from machine gun and artillery fire while ferrying personnel, cargo, and equipment to the beach. It took a real pounding, but with all the cosmetic surgery from the shipyard crews, it shined like a new penny.

***

The Allies had declared the island of Okinawa secured by 23 June with no end of the war in sight. We had heard horror stories that the Kamikazes were even worse than they had been in the waters of Iwo. Utilizing almost fifteen hundred planes, the Japanese either sank or put out of commission thirty US warships. Five LSMs were sunk and two severely damaged by suicide planes at Okinawa. One of those seven LSMs could have been us! If we hadn't have been so badly damaged at Iwo, we would have been at the landings at Okinawa as well. You learn to put things like that out of your mind.

During the first week of August, we took on provisions of food and ammunitions in preparation of the eventual invasion of the Japanese homeland. We ran practice beaching maneuvers on Red Beach #1 near Camp Pendleton as the *"Section II Unit Guide"* for the LSMs. To our great pleasure, we noticed the LST-477 was assigned as the *"Task Unit Guide"* in charge of the practice landings for our group of LSTs and LSMs. The hull of the 477 had been greatly improved since the Kamikaze attacks that it had sustained in the waters off Iwo Jima back in February. It was great to see that proud ship serving as our OTC (*Officer of Tactical Command*). It was also a matter of pride that we had been selected to lead the LSMs in the practice maneuvers as well. On 5 August we had gone through towing and fueling simulations with LST-477. When we untied from the 477, we returned to normal convoy position and prepared for gunnery exercises. During gunnery exercises, Verlin, Bill, and Jim expended sixteen hundred 20mm rounds, six hundred fifty .50 caliber rounds, and four hundred 40mm rounds. Our exercises also included laying smoke screens along Red Beach and loading cargo from AKAs. We took the mistakes of Iwo Jima and applied them to new techniques that we needed to test in California. With great reluctance, we were preparing to invade the home islands of Japan. It would be a fight to the death.

Over the radio on 7 August, Eldon had gotten the news that an "atomic bomb" had been dropped over Hiroshima, Japan the previous morning. Our B-17s had been bombing the Japanese homeland for months, and we all wondered what made this attack so different. We had no idea what an atomic bomb was except that it had the awesome power that practically vaporized the city and its inhabitants. We didn't get the full magnitude of this news until we learned of the second bomb of its kind that had been dropped over Nagasaki with similar results on 9 August. President Truman announced his hopes that these attacks would finally put an end this awful war. I prayed he was right.

Americans, especially those who didn't fight the Japanese, are quick to say that the atomic bombs were unnecessary and an evil deed. I'm not saying it was a wonderful thing that so many civilians were completely wiped out in two days of bombing. Our young boys were dying every day to stop the Japanese aggressive movement across the Pacific as the Japanese military murdered and enslaved the inhabitants of

Pacific Islands. Probably the worst crime was the raping of Nanjing by the Japanese military. They raped, mutilated, and murdered women and young girls without any level of restraint. The Japanese government had their people so brainwashed into worshipping Emperor Hirohito, that every man, woman, and child was trained to fight until the last. Sherman's *"total war"* tactics helped to bring the Confederacy to its knees in 1865; the Atomic Bomb served the same purpose in 1945. I know I have quoted Sherman before. But, this sums up the feelings invoked when men are asked to fight a fanatical enemy: *"War is cruelty. There's no use trying to reform it. The crueler it is, the sooner it is over."*

As an eighteen year old sailor, I was just relieved that the war was finally coming to an end. We were jubilantly celebrating on deck. We weren't looking forward to landing on Japanese beaches and facing the onslaught that would be waiting for us. We had survived Iwo Jima. I'm not sure how fortunate we would have been sliding the LSM-143 on the beaches of Honshu with the well deck full of Marines. We knew that there would be hundreds of thousands of casualties. Those would have included Allied military, Japanese military, and armed civilians. Most of those civilians would have included women and children who were told to die for honor of family and their "Emperor god". It would have been a gut-wrenching bloodbath like nothing we had ever seen.

I feel horrible regret for both sides now that I have had

years to reflect. I believe, also, that modern Japanese and those that had a chance to ponder on the events of the war feel the same remorse. Japan is a beautiful country with beautiful people, and I am so thankful that we are faithful allies today.

Chapter 12

CALM BEFORE THE STORM

"VJ Day", 2 September 1945, was proclaimed officially by President Truman when the ceremony was performed on the battleship USS Missouri. The war was over! However, the actual surrender announcement was made in America on 14 August 1945 and in Japan on 15 August when Japan accepted the terms of the Potsdam Declaration. The LSM-143 was in dry dock receiving its final repairs for our expected invasion of Japan that, thankfully, never happened. I didn't drink, but I was on liberty that day in San Francisco when we heard the news. There was utter pandemonium. The cars in the streets were honking their horns. The church bells were ringing. The ships out in the harbor were blowing fog horns. It was the sweetest sound I had ever heard. I could have had a girlfriend

WHAT PAY DOES A NAVY **WAVE** GET?

RATE	Monthly Base Pay-Clear	Food Allowance	Quarters Allowance	Total Monthly Income
Apprentice Seaman	$50.00	$54.00	$37.50	$141.50
Seaman Second Class	54.00	54.00	37.50	145.50
Seaman First Class	66.00	54.00	37.50	157.50
Petty Officers	78.00 & 126.00	54.00	37.50	169.50 & 217.50

*(Unless food and quarters are provided by Navy)

PLUS $3.00 for clothing, the finest medical and dental care, special tax exemption, low-cost Government life insurance, and free mail, reduced rates on transportation, theater tickets, etc.

anywhere I turned. There was a bunch of Navy WAVES (*Women Accepted for Volunteer Emergency Service*) waving their hats and skipping and twirling in the streets. Well, I teamed up with one of the WAVES, and we went marching down Main Street. Wow, the end of the war only happens once in a lifetime. Nothing ever came of that. I don't even know who she was except she was a woman somewhere near my age. We were both celebrating, and we just linked arms and went right down Main Street. It was so loud that if I had asked for her name, I probably couldn't have heard it anyway.

On 16 August, we were underway to Pearl Harbor in preparation to join the US occupational task force of the Japanese mainland. We had orders to go back out to sea. We weren't very happy about that. We were less happy when we

learned we were going to Japan. During the journey we kept sharp just in case the Japanese still had renegade forces who were not aware of the end of the war. The stern vibrated and shook the entire trip. Even with the engines all ahead full, the ship was not reaching its full ahead speed. We were, once again, suspicious that the propellers were out of alignment. If the propellers are out of line, the speed will suffer.

We arrived in Pearl on 25 August to take on fresh water, fuel, provisions, and "minor" repairs. The following afternoon, the divers went down to evaluate the condition of the screws. They reported that a couple of blades on our port propeller were bent and that there were leaks around the skegs. To the captain's dismay, we were placed into the dry dock of AFDL 23, Berth Able 15 to take care of the damage. The yard workers began the next day repairing the leaks in the port and starboard skegs and straightening the port propeller. Here we go again!

In hopeful optimism of all repairs, we proceeded from Pearl Harbor on 4 September to Saipan in convoy with LSM Flotilla 15 consisting of fifteen LSMs with ours included. We were escorted by the destroyer USS Poole (DE-151) and the sub chaser (PC-1185). The mechanics at Pearl must have done their jobs because the engines ran as smooth as they were when they were new. The vibration was gone, and we were heading out at eleven knots with both engines at standard speed. We had tested all ahead full with a result of thirteen knots but the captain decided not to hold that for long. We arrived in Saipan on 17 September to refuel. The LSM-143 also loaded aboard the 767th tank battalion of the US Army's 98th Division along with five Sherman tanks. The battalion was destined for Osaka, Japan as part of the US occupational forces.

General Quarters!

After three days, we joined a huge armada of LSTs, LCIs, LSMs and hundreds of war ships enroute to Japan. We were still in company of the same LSMs and escorts on our voyage to Japan as our trip to Saipan. We set a course at eleven and a half knots with our engines ahead at standard speed. On 26 September, we sighted the Shiono Misaki lighthouse on Honshu at 2205 hours. Radar reported that we were twenty-five miles from our landing zone at Wakayama.

In the early morning hours of 27 September, we laid in wait in the LSM anchorage just off the coast of Wakayama, Honshu, Japan. At 1000 hours, we were ordered to beach at our landing zone of Blue Beach #2 with five hundred feet of cable from the stern anchor. We maintained our engines at one third speed and filled the outer ballasts to keep the stern straight while the 767th Tank Battalion disembarked and unloaded their tanks and cargo. We spent the next three days unloading rolling stock from the AKA-46 to Blue Beach #2 until we were ordered to our next destination. We weren't allotted liberty to leave the ship on Honshu, so we just looked ahead to our next stop. I never, actually, stepped foot on Japanese soil. However, the LSM-143 got to touch the sand a few times. I guess that was good enough.

We received our orders on 1 October and were enroute to Okinawa by 1700 hours. We were in company of seven other LSMs and four LSTs. Our escorts for this passage were the subchasers USS PC-1128 and USS PC-576. We kept with the convoy by keeping our engines at two-thirds speed the entire time. We arrived in Buckner Bay near the Ryukyu Island of Okinawa at 0730 hours on 5 October. We anchored in the southernmost part of Buckner Bay at what was referred to at the time as "Red Entrance Buoy". We rotated duties as usual until the morning of 7 October when we weighed anchor and moored alongside the fuel oiler USS Camel (IX-113). After taking on twenty-four thousand gallons, we proceeded port side of the USS LSM-437. There, we took on fresh store for our general mess. We were able to get REAL fresh eggs (*not the powdered stuff*), beef, ham, lamb, veal, pork chops, sausage, turkey, and chicken. It was a smorgasbord.

***

"Buckner Bay" was the nickname used by United States military for Nakagusuka Bay after the Allies secured the island of Okinawa. It was coined so in memory of the commander of US land forces, Lieutenant General Simon Buckner who was killed in June 1945. Nakagusuka Bay lies off the southeastern coast of Okinawa with the town of Nakagusuka situated in the center.

***

The Japanese were not the only dangers lurking in the Pacific. We had stamped out that menace. Mother Nature felt the need to deliver her own brand of hell. One month after the surrender of Japan, a typhoon was warned to be in the Okinawa area at full force by 9 October 1945. This typhoon was to be known as *"Louise"* by meteorologists and had a devastating effect on the US Naval operations in Okinawa. Being one of the worst typhoons in history, with winds reaching one hundred twenty knots (*one hundred thirty-eight mph*) and seas as high as seventy feet, "Louise" did not stick with normal patterns that meteorologists had previously predicted. Therefore, it caught the Navy in this usually safe Buckner Bay by surprise, and left them no time to put their ships out to clear the storm. Ships of all sizes were packed into the bay, and the men were left to quickly batten down and secure their vessels for the storm.

Sometime on the morning of 6 October, Eldon Hibbard had picked up typhoon storm warnings on the radio while we were anchored near the Chinen Peninsula. The storm was three hundred fifty miles northwest of Saipan and was heading in a northwest direction at fifteen knots. This predicted path would send the typhoon several miles south of Okinawa toward Taiwan just as the typhoon on 29 September had done. As a precaution, we were warned to anchor and batten down in Buckner Bay.

Ships in the area were given the option to either make a run for it or anchor in the bay. Well, the LSM-143 had a top speed of 13.3 knots, but typhoon "Louise" would easily push in excess of eighty knots (*ninety-two mph*). The only option was clear. In the afternoon of 7 October, we were ordered to secure all gear aboard ship in preparation for the approaching typhoon. At 1730 hours, we left the southern area of Buckner Bay to the "northern typhoon anchorage" as it was called. This was an area just south of the Katchen Peninsula at the northernmost section of the bay some eighty miles north of our original anchorage which was near the Chinen Peninsula. The Katchen Peninsula was thought to be a safer anchorage in that the extended land mass could possibly provide extra protection from the high winds. I am not sure that it made any difference at all. We just followed orders and anchored in seven fathoms of water with forty-two fathoms of chain to the bow anchor. This anchorage was near the mountainous Katchen Peninsula, and appeared to offer some additional protective qualities. Part of it was deep water; part of it was not; part of it was maybe three or four feet deep. We let go of both of our anchors. The LSM-143 had a two ton anchor on the stern and a five hundred pounder on the bow. We weren't very concerned on the seventh because we were told it would pass way to our south.

The wind had died down some, but at around 0830 hours on 8 October, Eldon had received warnings that the storm had changed directions and was predicted to strike very close to southern Okinawa. By midafternoon at 1500 hours, the wind had increased to force six and the barometer had dropped to 29.14 inches of mercury. The warnings began to increase in frequency as the storm loomed ever closer.

Overnight and into the early hours of 9 October, the winds increased steadily. By 1000 hours the wind had risen to forty knots, and the barometer was down to 28.80, visibility was less than eight hundred yards. The seas were rising, and the rain was coming down in torrents, mixed with salt spray from the sea. I had been ordered to hoist the "whole gale" warning flags. These were two square flags, red with black squares in the center, hoisted one above the other that indicated the approach of a tropical hurricane, or an extremely severe or dangerous storm. We were having fun topside at first. We would lean against the wind with all of our weight, and it would hold us up. That fun lasted until it got to where we had to hang on to anything nearby for dear life. We realized it was time to go below decks and batten down. But, I had to get back to the conn with the officer on deck until ordered otherwise.

By noon, visibility was zero, and the wind was sixty knots from the east and northeast, with tremendous seas breaking over the ships. Small craft were already being torn loose from their anchors, and larger ships were desperately holding by aid of their engines. At 1400, the wind had risen to eighty knots, with gusts of greater intensity. The rain that drove in horizontally was more salt than fresh, and even the large ships were dragging anchor under the pounding of thirty to thirty-five foot waves. The bay was almost in total darkness, and during the mayhem, ships suddenly collided, or barely escaped colliding by the skillful use of engines, and were as quickly separated by the heavy seas. Scores of craft were blown ashore, and many were thrown onto the beach in one giant heap of metal. Crews worked feverishly to keep their vessels watertight and to secure a line to anything in an attempt to stop the collisions. Many ships had to be abandoned. Sometimes the crews were taken aboard by other ships; more often they made their way ashore, where they spent a miserable night huddled in caves and fields. Sailors were killed or missing in the waylay.

By 1600 the typhoon reached its peak, with steady winds of one hundred knots and frequent gusts of one hundred twenty knots. At that time, the barometer dipped to 28.20. That was the lowest reading that the barometers recorded, and was probably the point of passage of the center of the typhoon, but the maximum winds continued unabated for another two hours, the gusts becoming fiercer, if anything. During that period, the wind shifted to the north, then to the northwest, and began to blow ships back off the west and north reefs of the bay across to the south, and sometimes dragging anchor the entire way. The wild voyages by damaged ships caused a nightmarish series of collisions and near escapes with other drifting ships and shattered hulks.

Gales of wind rushed and waves lashed over the entire topside of the LSM-143, including the conning tower where I was stationed. At 1616 hours, we had let out an additional one hundred feet of cable to the stern anchor. The wind was dragging those anchors and blowing us and we dragged bottom. We left the radio on full broadcast. Ships would identify themselves saying, *"Help! We're sinking!"* Men were terror stricken, and pleading for help from someone because they were being battered and sinking. We heard too much of that. We heard someone ask for help, and then, all of the sudden in the middle of the passage, it would go blank. We heard lots of messages for help, but we were powerless to give any assistance.

The LSM-143, and several other vessels, was dragged along the Negress reef. Distress calls include a log recording that read: *"0807 V LSM 143 BT We are on Negress Reef berth 125"*. We were scraping along and losing our bottom. You could hear it scrape… scrape… scrape… crunch… crunch; our lower decks were flooded. We had a lot of water below our compartment decks. We had rocks and reefs that had come up through our floor. We had to walk around that reef that stuck up through the bottom. Of course, water was sloshing around.

At 1650 hours, the LSM-143 was out of control when it came down hard onto the reef bow first. We ran both engines at two-thirds, and barely avoided a collision with a large repair ship, the USS Mona Island (ARG-9), already aground. The PC-590 was blown aground on the opposite side of Negress Reef from the 143 and just forward of the bow of ARG-9. The YMS-146 also was washed onto the reef astern of 143 and just forward of the bow of ARG-9.

Eldon heard a distress message over the radio from the YMS-146.

"YMS-146 is taking on water. We are astern of the 143! We are in need of assistance!"

At the same time, the minesweeper's signalman was flashing his Aldis lamp toward me with the distress signal. He signaled that the ship was breaking apart and taking on water. Realizing the ship's perilous situation, Lieutenant White ordered,

"Garforth! Tell them we are bringing their crew aboard!"

I flashed a signal to the ship to *"stand clear, we are mooring alongside"*. We had very little control of where we were going alongside this ship. We were completely at the mercy of the gale-force wind. The bottom scraped and tore along the reef. The hull moaned and creaked as the seams stressed against the force of wind, sea, and coral. It resembled the sound of fingernails across a blackboard that my elementary teacher used to do to get our attention. We were blowing probably within a foot of this minesweeper and we stopped. It was a wooden Navy minesweeper. It was probably about one hundred yards that we scraped…scraped…scraped toward them and stopped. We placed our starboard quarter against the YMS-146's starboard quarter with approximately a ten foot overlap. All hands aboard the minesweeper were ordered to abandon ship. At 1657 hours, one of our crew was Basil Overton who helped tie the ship alongside the LSM-143. Basil was a hillbilly from Tennessee. He was about six foot three, two hundred and something pounds. The whole crew was on their deck, and Basil reached down there and picked every one of those guys aboard our ship. He would just grab them in a handshake fashion and heave each man over the side. There were thirty men and four officers. They would have all been killed. Both ships slid about twenty feet down the reef while all of this was happening. By 1710 hours, Basil pulled the last man aboard; the captain. This may sound hokey like a Hollywood movie. But, as soon as we loosened the ties from the minesweeper, it rocked a couple of times as it teetered atop the reef. Then, suddenly, it broke free from the reef and drifted away from us. We weren't more than a few yards away, when the YMS-146 totally disintegrated. They would have lost every man!

The bottom of the LSM-143 was practically destroyed

itself, and we were taking on water. At 1730 hours, we were thrown further upon the reef due to the force of wind and sea. In a futile attempt to hold fast, all bilges and tanks were deliberately flooded so as to set the ship firmly on the reef to ride out the typhoon. The ship was rocking a bit, but holding strong to the reef. We held our breath and prayed for the end of this horrifying storm. At that time, I was ordered to take shelter in the radio shack with Eldon Hibbard and a few other guys. I grabbed my handheld Aldis lamp so that I could signal if the need arose.

***

In another unselfish act of heroism, members of the ARG-9 shot a line with a boatswain chair to the distressing sub chaser PC-590 nearby. The signalman on the ARG-9 flashed the

message "stand clear" to the PC-590 with his Aldis lamp. The crew of the rescuing ship threw cargo nets over the side, but then thought better of the idea. They figured if the two ships collided with men on the nets, they would be crushed. The two ships were scraping along the reef at one hundred fifty feet at first. Then, they closed within one hundred feet. The two ships finally gained temporary stability on the reef with only fifty feet between them. With flood lights beaming, crew members pulled the sailors from the PC-590 to safety of the ARG-9 during the height of the typhoon. A few of us were taking shelter in the radio shack and had the door open to witness the crew of the ARG-9 in action. Those boys completely risked their lives to save every man from the faltering PC-590. The crew of the PC-590 shot a line across to the stern of the ARG-9 whose crew quickly retrieved and tied taut. A "breeches buoy" was fashioned along the three inch manila line, and the first man was sent across. It took about two minutes to send each man across the line. It seemed more like an hour as the storm built up force and became even more ferocious. Waves were slamming across the after deck where each man, soaked and dismayed, disembarked from the makeshift cradle. Meanwhile, two ammunition lockers broke free and slammed against the bulkhead just missing a crewman. The gales were so violent, that the remaining men were sent to the wheelhouse of the PC-590 to wait their turn to cross the line. This was done in spite of the advancing deterioration of the ship. Tending the line had become more perilous, and the rescuers nearly washed overboard. When the last officer was being brought across the breeches buoy, the line gave and he fell into the sea and sank immediately. We heard the crew scream "*Hold on!*" as they heaved the line with all their might.

The officer was heaved aboard and the line was cut. Within minutes, at 2015 hours, the PC-590 snapped in the increasing gale. The ship severed completely in half. Every man aboard the PC-590 was spared.

***

When I looked out to sea after the winds had subsided, the bay was a graveyard of twisted steel. There were LSTs with their bow doors warped and barely hanging from their hinges. The PC-590, what was left of it, was lying in a two distinct pieces on the reef. I never saw the minesweeper, YMS-146, again. We had witnessed it being slashed apart like a rag doll the night before. Unidentified debris floated in the wake. One item that will always stick in my mind was a signal flag waving on the surface of the water. It was snagged to the wreckage of the PC-590 and was just moving up and down with the waves of the sea. It seemed to me to be making a distress call, but instead was signaling that all was clear.

The shore was in disarray as well. The hood of a jeep was peeking out from underneath a ripped pile of tent material and boards. A two and a half ton six-by-six was turned over on its roof. Quonset huts and tents were torn to shreds and barracks were leveled to the ground. Metal frames and towers were twisted into unrecognizable shapes. The beach was littered with ships that had gone aground. Crews on the shore were already at work cleaning up the jumble of equipment and troop quarters. I had the same sick feeling that I had experienced after Iwo Jima. I just looked around and saw waste and destruction. We had also gotten news that several boys had lost their lives. Our Navy boys had performed exactly like this was a battle. It WAS a battle. We had to fight an adversary that was blowing us around the bay. Courageous action was all over that bay the night before I am sure of it. It's times like this that test a man's character. The men in that bay proved what it was like to be an American. The selflessness was everywhere. The men tossed around in that typhoon were willing to give all to save the lives of their comrades.

LSM-143 received major damage to her hull, engines, keel, structures, and her seaworthiness was questionable. We had also sustained leaks in the fuel tanks and the ballast tanks used to hold us down to the reef. When the storm subsided, dry dock ships were sent to rescue the LSM-143 from sinking. This floating dry dock could sink itself just enough to allow a troubled ship to pull into its dry dock area. Then, the water was released by pumps and the dry dock ship rose out of its descent. We weren't drivable; our whole bottom was gone. This time, we would have to be lowered into the dry dock. We ultimately ended up on the reef about to sink. Two pontoon barges pulled up on each side of us. Then, somehow, they got cables underneath from one barge to another barge. They had a winch that tightened up the cable and literally picked us up off the reef. Then, a tug pulled us onto the dry dock ship (ARD-27) which raised itself around us. Every place the Navy goes, they have hundreds of these floating docks officially referred to as an *"Auxiliary Repair Dock"*. We had been able to pull inside of the well decks of these floating dry docks under our own power. This time we needed help. While the ship was resting on the cradle, welders began to patch big chunks of steel to the bow.

From the day of the typhoon (9 October) to 14 October, we had shared the LSM-143 with the crew of the YMS-146. They were a gracious bunch of boys, and always appreciative. They made good conversation about life back home and the fate that almost took their young lives. But, at 1500 hours on 14 October, the crew of the former YMS-146 boarded the USS Sherburne (APA-205) to be taken to Pearl Harbor and reassigned to new duties with the US Navy.

The USS Sherburne was scheduled for duty in Operation Magic Carpet to return men back to the United States, but was sent to Okinawa on the 12 – 14 October to transport more than one thousand four hundred survivors of minesweepers and other ships destroyed during Typhoon Louise. Upon completion of this assignment, the APA-205 resumed its duties in support of Operation Magic Carpet.

By storm's end, a total of twelve ships and craft were sunk, two hundred twenty-two grounded, and thirty-two severely damaged. Casualties numbered at thirty-six killed, forty-seven missing and one hundred seriously injured. Practically all food, medical supplies and other stores were destroyed, and over eighty percent of all buildings were knocked down. Although repairable, over sixty planes were damaged.

If the war had not ended on 2 September, the damage, especially to the amphibious vessels, would have seriously impacted the plans for "Operation Olympic". Operation Olympic was the codename for the Allied invasion of the Japanese homeland that never materialized.

Chapter 13

GOING HOME

The dry dock in Buckner Bay did all they could do for us with their limited means. Most of the repairs performed on these ships were designed to "patch" the wounded ship, and get it back into operation as soon as possible. The dry docks were the "corpsmen" for the ships of the fleet. If a ship was "wounded", we called for the dry docks. The men on these dry docks were repairing ships day and night at Iwo, and also for several days after the typhoon. There never seemed to be enough of them. If we were damaged, we just had to bide our time until a dock had an available bay. After leaving a dry dock, we were always eventually sent to a naval repair base for more extensive repairs. They were better equipped than a dry dock due to their convenience to parts and supplies. The bases also had room for the more high tech equipment. The dry docks did their jobs. They were a vital asset to the fleet. We would have been rendered useless early on in the campaign for Iwo Jima if it weren't for them. The LSM-143 would have been scrapped immediately after Typhoon Louise if we could not have gotten those quick repairs.

0400 hours 30 October, I was relieved by George Cimbala for his four hour watch on the conn. We made our typical formal exchanges of the logs and messages, but he was a little melancholy. I inquired, *"George, what's eatin' you?"*

He replied, *"I've got enough points. I'm goin' home to Philly."*

"Good for you! When are you shipping out?"

"Tonight."

"That's great! What are you gonna do now?"

"Nothin' for now. But, I'm gonna use that GI Bill to go to school; make somethin' out of myself."

Then, George hesitated a moment, looked out into Buckner Bay, and continued with nostagia: *"Take care of my ship, Garforth. She's kept us safe. And, it's been my home so long, I didn't think it would be this hard to leave."*

"I feel the same way George. I think I'll stay with her for a while. It's been a pleasure serving with you. Have a safe trip."

We shook hands, and at 1825 hours that evening he and seven other sailors boarded a DUKW to shore. They would be discharged at the demobilization center on Okinawa, and then put on an APA enroute to the states.

We had a point system where we earned a point for every month of service. If we were on sea duty, we got extra points for that. I had more than enough points to have transferred to another ship to take me back to the states and be discharged. But, I thought if I'm going back to the states, I am going to go back on my own ship. What is the point in packing up all my gear and doing that? I wanted the LSM-143 to be the last thing I saw before I departed from the Navy. I owed her that much. Like George said, it had become home for all of us.

We remained in the dry dock for several days. Boredom sets in when a crew of boys are kept hulled up for too long. This is an incident that has to be shared because it is too funny to be true. But, when you are dealing with the military, sometimes their justice makes little sense. One of our boys decided that he would liberate a cake from the galley and hide it in his rack. Someone got wise to him, and he was brought in front of the captain in "deck court". The accused sailor was found guilty of *"illegal possession of cake"*, and was sentenced to a loss of twenty days' pay. It's even explicitly written in the deck log with that exact wording. On New Year's Day 1946, our new radioman was tried at Captain's Mass for the *"illegal purchase of one case of beer"* from the Ship's Service Stores. This *"purchase"* was made on New Year's Eve in order to make his season a little brighter. He sentence was a rating downgrade from S1c(RM) to S3c(RM). Shouldn't the person who sold it illegally have gotten tried as well? I'm perplexed.

The USS ARD-27 made solid repairs to the underside of the ship and, of course, the propellers. I lost count since Iwo Jima exactly how many new propellers were put on the LSM-143 or how many times they had been straightened. Losing a propeller is like losing your legs and feet. No matter how strong the engine was, the propellers had to be healthy. We were made waterborne once the repairs were complete on ARD-27, and were immediately sent to moor alongside the ARB-7 (Aristaeus Repair, Battle). This type of ship was designed to repair ships that had taken on damage during battle. Crews came aboard the LSM-143 to make various repairs of damage mostly sustained during the typhoon. We required more extensive repairs to the engines, radar and radio equipment, winches and anchors, and countless other issues. When repairs were complete, the crew chief said, *"This will get you to Pearl Harbor."*

But, before we would be sent to Pearl, we had some shore duty on Okinawa. We left the LSM-143 in its anchorage, and were transported to the mainland by DUKWs. We spent the majority of November giving aid to the cleanup and rebuilding efforts on the island. This place was a disaster area. I mean, it was a mess. Tents had to be erected again. Vehicles had to be righted back to their wheels. The beach was so entirely clogged with wreckage that we had to be resupplied by air drops from C-47s. Four sailors from a destroyed ship came aboard and were added to our muster roll. These boys were taking the duties of the guys who were discharged with George Cimbala.

On 26 November 1945, we were on our way to Hagushi, Okinawa to rendezvous with a group of other LSMs to convoy to the Marianas Islands. Our convoy included LSMs 468, 206, and LSM-48 towing LSM-265 suffering from engine failure.

Going Home

Our ship would be in the lead with Lieutenant White as Officer of Tactical Command (OTC). We ran the engines at two-thirds for the first three days, and then took over the towing duties on 30 November for the remainder of the voyage. We were forced to halt the convoy in order to repair the rudder angle indicator on our ship. Then, to delay our trip even more, the towing bridle on the LSM-265 gave way and had to be welded back three times during the next three days. Finally, in the early morning hours of 6 December, we arrived in Apra Harbor, Guam. We had spent a lot of time at Apra Harbor before the Battle of Iwo Jima. It was almost exactly a year ago that we had pulled into Apra Harbor, slid onto the beach, and unloaded those nasty creosote poles we had hauled all the way from Oakland, California. The following month, mid-January, we loaded the mine men destined for *Operation Starvation*, and delivered them to Tinian in the Marianas Island group. Apra Harbor was also the rendezvous point for LSM Group Fourteen to assemble with the rest of the fleet to depart for "*Island X*". All of these memories ran through my mind as we pulled into the harbor.

The newly promoted Lieutenant John A Merschel, a fellow Michigan boy, took over command of the LSM-143 on 11 December. Lieutenant White had enough points to discharge and was onboard the next APA to the states and to his home in New York.

The Seabees installed refrigerators to our after tank deck

while we were docked in Saipan on 19 December. During the next month, we served as a reefer ship to ferry supplies, food, and equipment between Guam, Saipan, and Tinian. It was business as usual except for one more special Christmas dinner whipped up by the galley. We made landings on the beaches to deliver construction supplies, or we would moor alongside an APA to offload food and equipment.

Along the way several crewman decided that it was time to cash in their service points and head home. James Romano and Basil Overton transferred to the USS Haverfield (DE-393) while we were moored off Saipan, and Ensign Bryan discharged on one of our stops back to Guam. This left the ship in command of the newly promoted Lieutenant Merschel.

With a brief stop at Eniwetok Atoll from 20 – 31 January 1946, two USCG fireboats were loaded into our well deck with the US Coast Guard crew also aboard. On the early morning of 31 January, we pulled out of Eniwetok on our way to Pearl Harbor. The 143 arrived in Pearl Harbor on 8 February and stayed in dry dock until 21 February. We took further repairs at Pearl Harbor until finally pulling out on 6 March, 1946. The LSM-143 was patched up enough at Pearl to get back to the states.

The final leg to San Francisco started on 6 March accompanied by PC-1141 and APC-108. About halfway across the Pacific, the APC-108 stopped abruptly after suffering major engine failure. We took the ship in tow and the convoy was able to limp the rest of the journey. Several hundred miles west of California, our power steering failed and she was manually steered on home. We, once again, passed the Farallon and Alcatraz Islands knowing that we were close to home. As much as we prayed, Murphy's Law ruled our last few steps toward shore. Just a few miles from the Golden Gate Bridge both engines became inoperative and, while adrift, tugs directed by the harbor pilot took control of the ship through San Francisco Bay. When we became closer to San Francisco Bay, I was the first to see the bridge come barely into view just over the horizon. I looked down at Verlin Smith who was busy cleaning the 40mm gun mount for what would probably be the very last time.

"Hey Verlin!"

"Yeah! What is it Garforth?"

I pointed to the horizon and shouted, *"Golden Gate in '46!"*

Verlin straightened from his stooped position at his gun mount and took a long, deep breath. After taking a moment to absorb the beauty of that wonderful bridge, he shook his head and smirked, *"You're not much of a poet Garforth! But, that's the best line I've ever heard."*

I realized that my feeble attempt at a comedic line didn't rhyme, but I knew that I had to beat Verlin to the punch. Our entire crew had made it "back alive in '45". We were all relieved to be "out of the sticks in '46". If it wasn't for the Atomic Bomb, there is no telling how long the Japanese would have dragged out this horrible conflict. It wouldn't have just been "Golden Gate in '48". It would have been "'49", "'50", or "'51". Who knows how long the fight would have lasted. We were heading home. The war was over.

The LSM-143 took its final docking at Hunters Point, California on 17 March 1946. Our final duty was to unload the Coast Guard crew and their fireboats. Lieutenant Merschel was discharged upon arrival leaving the command of the LSM-143 to Lieutenant James Juliana. Juliana would only enjoy his command of the ship until April Fool's Day when he was discharged and shipped home to New Jersey. We went through two other commanding officers until the decommissioning of the ship. On 25 April, 1946, an inspection party of three officers came aboard from the Industrial Manager's office to determine whether the ship should go out as scrap or if it could be salvaged. I left the ship before I could find out the final fate of the 143. I had heard later that the USS LSM-143 was towed to the Mare Island Navy Yard in Vallejo, California where she was decommissioned on 14 June 1946. The ship moored in the harbor for seven months awaiting its future.

In February 1947, she was sold to the Elliot Chemical Cleaning Company of San Francisco, California. Beyond that, no one knows what has become of the ship, but she and her crew served the US Navy well during her brief combat tour in the Pacific. No matter where it lies now, above or below the water's surface, the LSM-143 will always have a place to sail in my heart and my soul.

EPILOGUE

I left the war with the rating of Signalman Second Class. I was offered the patch with three stripes, but I turned down the Signalman First Class rating and never sewed them on my uniform. I didn't want to get shore duty. If I couldn't be on the water, I was going home. I said to myself, *"I'm destined to go home as soon as we get back to the states. I'm gone!"* I had an option of taking my discharge in the port of San Francisco or in Chicago. I chose to go on home and take my discharge in Chicago.

A troop train from San Francisco left on its way to Chicago with hundreds of us Navy men. Now, I was a petty officer on ship, so I never had to sand a rust spot or swab the deck. We had escaped all of that duty on ship because we were petty officers. They had a regular galley set up on this troop train. Since we had been petty officers, we were chosen to dispense the food on the train. I had a real tough job in the galley. I had a tub with ice cold fresh water and quarters of butter and a fork with the tines bent down. I would fish out the butter and flick it onto the trays as the men came by. Anyway, I had it pretty good right to the end.

When we were just outside of Chicago in the country, they ordered us to throw out all the food we hadn't used on the trip. They opened the boxcar doors while we were still motoring at forty miles per hour, and we threw out butter, meat, and everything else. The Navy bases at Great Lakes didn't want any food that had come off of a troop train. They only wanted food that would have arrived fresh. We all knew someone who could have used that food. It was such a waste.

I was discharged when I arrived in Chicago in June 1946. I was fortunate enough to be able to drive my Grandpa's Model A at the age of fourteen and receive my first driver's license. When I got off the bus in Fountain, my Grandpa presented me with this same car I had driven before the war. At that time, there wasn't a used car to be found. So my granddad said, *"You might as well have the old Ford because I am too old to drive it anyway."*

My lifelong desire was to be a carpenter apprentice just like the Grandpa I so deeply adored. I was a do-it-yourselfer. I could do plumbing, electrical, gardening, and carpentry. I was just a "Jack-of-all-trades" and "Master of None" you might say. However, with nothing available, the closest thing the employment office had to a carpenter's job was a lumber yard loader. I had worked too long for "peanuts" in that lumber yard unloading box cars. This job involved forty-four hours a week at ninty cents an hour which wore out a lot of clothes. My spare time in church would be pulling out slivers of wood from my hands. It wasn't pennies from heaven, but it kept us afloat until I could find something better.

With four children, it was difficult to make ends meet. We couldn't survive on ninety cents an hour. Even back then, the cost of living meant that I was practically working for nothing.

GM DIESEL

7-28-59

So, in 1951, at the employment office once again, I was told about an opening at General Motors. In the 1950's there were no personal protective equipment requirements; therefore my hearing was damaged from working in a high noise environment. For thirty-one years I worked in research and development on diesel injection systems, contributing mostly by training my own supervisors.

One of my good buddies at GM was in the 28th Regiment of the 5th Marine Division during the war. He was a guy that I met after the war. Leonard Keith Stratton and I were working mates for thirty-one years at GM. He hated the name "Leonard", so he went by "Keith". His job was altogether different than mine. He was an operator of the diesel engines that were tested. We did everything together. We would have family get-togethers independent of work. So I had a personal experience with Keith; he was a close friend. I never had any brothers, but he was about the same thing. He just died not very long ago. When one loses someone that is that close it's just like losing a brother. We were both at Iwo Jima at the same time. Of course, I never knew him then. I didn't even know he was on Iwo Jima until we started working together at GM. I always wondered, but never thought to ask, if he was one of the over nine hundred Marines that we picked up at the end of the battle. I might have looked right at him and didn't know it. They never told us what regiment they were from. Keith used to kid me and say, *"The Marines have servants, and they are called the Navy"*. There was always a little bit of rivalry amongst the branches of service, but we had each other's back when the chips were down. The Marines always did a real service to give our men some help every time some of them were on board. They were tough, and we respected them. We did everything we could to always get them to the beach as safely as possible. I think, for that reason, they respected us as well.

Today, I live in McMinnville, Tennessee with my wife, Annabelle. She and I travel from time to time, visiting my five daughters in Grand Rapids, Michigan. We have even traveled recently through the Panama Canal. We traveled through the locks on a cruise ship into Lake Gatun. Then, the ship turned around to go back through the locks toward the Atlantic. On our way back to the US mainland, we were able to visit the beautiful, pristine islands of San Blas. Look these islands up sometime on the internet; they are beautiful. This was a much more relaxed trip through the Panama Canal than the last time I made the trip back in 1944.

My time in the Navy was just a drop in the bucket compared to the years I have spent on this Earth. But, those years formed me. They helped to make me the man that I am today. When a man survives war, he looks at things differently. Men are more sensitive to the things that they dared to take for granted beforehand. The grass is a greener color and it smells great when it is cut. The sky is a shade bluer and the clouds slide across like floating cotton. The nighttime sounds of the cicadas create a soothing music that is best enjoyed when the windows are open on a cool summer evening. The people in my life are more precious. Time is more precious. I intend not to waste a single second—and I haven't.

Stand Navy out to sea, Fight our Battle Cry;
We'll never change our course,
So vicious foe you steer shy-y-y-y.
Roll out the TNT, Anchors Aweigh. Sail on to Victory
And sink their bones to Davy Jones, Hooray!

Anchors Aweigh, my boys, Anchors Aweigh.
Farewell to foreign shores,
We sail at break of day-ay-ay-ay.
Through our last night on shore, Drink to the foam,
Until we meet once more.
Here's wishing you a happy voyage home.

Blue of the Mighty Deep; Gold of God's Great Sun
Let these colors be till all of time be done, done, done,
On seven seas we learn Navy's stern call:
Faith, Courage, Service true,
with Honor, Over Honor, Over All.

-   *"Anchors Aweigh" lyrics by Alfred Hart Miles;*
   musical composition by Charles A Zimmerman,
   Music Director, US Naval Academy, 1906

BIBLIOGRAPHY

(1) Garforth, Delmor Dean; Signalman 2nd Class; USN; USS LSM-143; June 1944 – December 1946.

(2) http://www.history.navy.mil/faqs/faq102-6.htm

(3) O'Neill, Richard; *Suicide Squads: The Men and Machines of World War II Special Operations* (The Lyons Press, 2001), p.237

(4) Ace Collins (2003), *Stories Behind the Hymns That Inspire America*, Grand Rapids, Mich.: Zondervan, pp. 153–154

(5) Photo: http://www.latinworld.com/tag/san-blas-islands

(6) The diary of James N. Juliana, USNR, USS LSM-143

(7) Photos: http://www.navsource.org/archives/10/14/14143.htm

(8) Photo: http://www.usni.org/heritage/slideshows/iwo-jima

(9) Photo: http://en.wikipedia.org/wiki/File:WAVES_recruitment_poster.jpg

(10)   http://www.lighthousefriends.com/lake_mi.html

(11)   http://njscuba.net/artifacts/ship_lightship.html

(12)   Salecker, Gene; *The Second Pearl Harbor: The West Loch Disaster, May 21, 1944* (University of Oklahoma Press, 2014)

(13)   Deck log, LSM-143, June 30, 1944 – December 1946, National Archives, College Park, MD

(14)   Deck log, LST-477, February 21, 1945 – February 23, 1945, National Archives, College Park, MD

(15)   Deck log, LST-809, February 21, 1945 – February 23, 1945, National Archives, College Park, MD

(16)   Deck log, LSD-2 "USS Belle Grove", March 12, 1945 – March 13, 1945, National Archives, College Park, MD

(17)   Deck log, APA-160 "USS Deuel", February 26, 1945 – February 27, 1945, National Archives, College Park, MD

(18)   Deck log, LST-646, February 24, 1945 – February 25, 1945, National Archives, College Park, MD

(19)   Deck log, LST-944, February 23, 1945 – February 24, 1945, National Archives, College Park, MD

(20)   Deck log, AKN-4 "USS Keokuk", February 19,

1945 – February 25, 1945, National Archives, College Park, MD

(21)   Deck log, LST-943, February 20, 1945 – February 25, 1945, National Archives, College Park, MD

(22)   Deck log, AKA-116, February 21, 1945 – February 26, 1945, National Archives, College Park, MD

(23)   Deck log, AKA-64, February 25, 1945 – February 28, 1945, National Archives, College Park, MD

(24)   Deck log, AKA-90, March 1, 1945 – March 3, 1945, National Archives, College Park, MD

(25)   Deck log, AKA-93, March 1, 1945 – March 3, 1945, National Archives, College Park, MD

(26)   Deck log, AKA-67, March 2, 1945 – March 4, 1945, National Archives, College Park, MD

(27)   Deck log, USS Cape Isabel, March 4, 1945 – March 7, 1945, National Archives, College Park, MD

(28)   Deck log, USS Kingsport Victory, March 6, 1945 – March 9, 1945, National Archives, College Park, MD

(29)   Deck log, YSM-146, October 5, 1945 – October 11, 1945, National Archives, College Park, MD

(30)   Deck log, PC-590, October 5, 1945 – October

11, 1945, National Archives, College Park, MD

(31)   Deck log, ARG-9, October 5, 1945 – October 11, 1945, National Archives, College Park, MD

(32)   Deck log, ARD-27, October 5, 1945 – October 11, 1945, National Archives, College Park, MD

(33)   Action Report, LSM-143, 9 March 1945, National Archives, College Park, MD

(34)   https://sites.google.com/site/usskeokuk/damageatiwojima

(35)   Photo: 3rd Tank Battalion Iwo Jima from LST-477, http://www.ww2gyrene.org/Tanks_Image_Gallery_3.html#third

(36)   Hata, Ikuhiko, and Yasuho Izawa. 1989. *Japanese Naval Aces and Fighter Units in World War II*. Translated by Don Cyril Gorham. Originally published in 1970 by Kantosha in Japanese. Annapolis, MD: Naval Institute Press.

(37)   Inoguchi, Rikihei, and Tadashi Nakajima. 1958. *The Divine Wind: Japan's Kamikaze Force in World War II*. Annapolis: Naval Institute Press.

(38)   Osuo, Kazuhiko. 2005. *Tokubetsu kougekitai no kiroku (kaigun hen) (Record of special attack corps (Navy))*. Tokyo: Kojinsha.

(39)   Tokkotai Senbotsusha Irei Heiwa Kinen Kyoukai (Tokkotai Commemoration Peace

Memorial Association). 1990. *Tokubetsu Kougekitai (Special Attack Corps)*. Tokyo: Tokkotai Senbotsusha Irei Heiwa Kinen Kyoukai.

(40)   Warner, Denis, Peggy Warner, with Commander Sadao Seno. 1982. *The Sacred Warriors: Japan's Suicide Legions*. New York: Van Nostrand Reinhold.

(41)   Yasunobu, Takeo. 1972. *Kamikaze Tokkoutai (Kamikaze special attack corps)*. Edited by Kengo Tominaga. Tokyo: Akita Shoten.

(42)   https://marines.togetherweserved.com/usmc/ser vlet/tws.webapp.WebApp?cmd=ShadowBoxProfile&ty pe=Person&ID=185363

(43)   Hibbard, Eldon J.; Radioman Second Class; United States Navy; USS LSM-143. June 1944-December 1946.

(44)   Hornfischer, James D.; *The Last Stand of the Tin Can Sailors: The Extraordinary World War II Story of the US Navy's Finest Hour*; (Bantam Books, 2005).

(45)   Sheftall, M. G.; *Blossoms in the Wind: Human Legacies of the Kamikaze*; (NAL Books, 2005)

(46)   US Coast Guard; *The Coast Guard at War, Volume VII: Lost Cutters*. Washington, DC: Historical Section, Public Information Division, US Coast Guard

Headquarters. July 1, 1947. Pages 26-30.

(47)   Mair, Michael; *Kaiten: Japan's Secret Manned Suicide Submarine and the First American Ship it Sank in WWII*; (Berkley, 2015)